Land Law
2020/2021 - *Simply Notes*

CONTENTS

What is this book?   i

1   Introduction to Land Law   1

2   Estates and Interests in Land   Pg 7

3   Registered and Unregistered Title   Pg 16

4   Freehold Covenants   Pg 26

5   Easements and Profits   Pg 35

6   Mortgages   Pg 49

7   Proprietary Estoppel   Pg 57

8   Trusts of Land   Pg 62

9   Trusts of the Home   Pg 66

10   Common Ownership   Pg 77

11   Leases   Pg 87

12   Adverse Possession   Pg 99

WHAT IS THIS BOOK?

1. It is a simple and straightforward introduction to land law.
2. It is an up-to-date set of law subject notes.
3. It is a book designed to give you a quick and accessible knowledge of the law in a particular area of your course of study, before you move on to more complex texts.
4. It is suitable for students studying LLB, GDL, LLM/MA law conversion courses, PGDL, or CILEx qualifications.
5. It is a book which is not a replacement for hard work and dedication to the programme of study you have embarked on.

CHAPTER 1
INTRODUCTION TO LAND LAW

Introduction: What is land law all about?

1.01 Land Law is all about rights: Identifying rights; creating rights; and, protecting rights, in relation to land. The rights which exist in relation to land vary greatly, with some being more significant than others; some are major, and some are minor. The methods by which these rights can be created also vary, with some requiring strict formality (which usually means some form of writing), while other rights can be created informally by the behaviour of the parties.

1.02 As if this weren't (seemingly) complicated enough, there are schemes of protection for these rights which might, ultimately, mean whether the rights are binding on, ie, enforceable against, others. However, this wider picture is for later in the book. The first stage in understanding land law, is understanding the **definition of land**.

What is land? How is it defined?

1.03 It is important to know what constitutes 'land' before considering other parts of land law. An adequate definition of land is valuable because it sets down the extent of an individual's rights over property. However, a definition of land is also important for the tax man (who can levy stamp duty) and the mortgagee (a bank or building society) who might repossess the land.

Statutory Definition

1.04 Section 205(1)(ix), Law of Property Act 1925 contains a definition of 'land'. The definition, which is not exhaustive, states that land *includes* land of any tenure (freehold or leasehold), mines and minerals, buildings or parts of buildings and other corporeal hereditaments; also rent and other incorporeal hereditaments, and easements, rights, privileges, or benefits relating to land. These are the key parts of the statute. It is clear this is not a full definition. For the rest of the definition, it is necessary to turn to the common law.

Above and Below the Ground

1.05 The basic common law position is rather crudely summed up by the Latin maxim *cuius est solum eius est usque ad coelum et ad inferos* – he who owns the land, owns everything below the land and everything above it up to the heavens. However, this maxim is only part of the story and doesn't accurately reflect the law.

Above the Ground

1.06 A landowner does not enjoy ownership of all the space above their land. The extent of their enjoyment is limited to that which is necessary for the ordinary use and enjoyment of the land and any structures on it. The distinction is between the lower and upper strata of airspace; the lower is the landowner's (**Kelsen v Imperial Tobacco Co (1957)**), the upper is not (**Bernstein of Leigh (Baron) v Skyviews & General Ltd (1978)**). The lower strata is probably the first 200m above the ground (Rules of Air Regulations 1996).

1.07 In **Kelsen v Imperial Tobacco Co (1957)**, an advertising sign projected a few inches into the airspace above the landowner's shop. This was held to interfere with the landowner's property rights and a ordered its removal from the airspace. Similarly, in **Laiqat v Majid (2005)**, an extractor fan was erected which projected 75cm into the landowner's garden at a height of 4.5m, also had to be removed. Contrasting these **Bernstein of Leigh (Baron) v Skyviews and General Ltd (1978)** where the defendant flew over the landowner's property and took a photograph. The landowner claimed it was a trespass, but given it was high above the land, it was not a trespass.

Commercial aircraft

1.08 Section 76(1), Civil Aviation Act 1982 gives immunity from trespass or nuisance where the aeroplane is sufficiently high above ground, accounting for the weather, etc, as is reasonable.

Below the Ground

1.09 A land owner will enjoy the right to anything which is under the land he owns (**Waverley BC v Fletcher (1996)**), unless there is a statutory or common law rule which takes it from him!

1.10 Minerals and other similar substances *generally* form part of the estate of the landowner and he is able to treat them as his own. However, coal belongs to the Coal Authority (Coal Industry Act 1994) and oil and natural gas to the Crown (Petroleum Act 1998).

1.11 The Crown, by prerogative, has the right to mines of gold and silver. In addition, where items found are classed as treasure under the Treasure Act 1996, these vest in the Crown.

1.12 All other items found in the below the ground of the landowner belong to the landowner. In **Waverley BC v Fletcher (1996)**, the defendant, while on council land, found a medieval brooch approximately nine inches below the surface. The coroner held that it was not treasure trove, so the question of ownership arose. The CA held that the brooch belonged to the council. Had the item been found on the ground, the landowner would have to show an intention to manifest control of the area where the item was found in order to keep it. This was held in **Parker v British Airways Board (1982)**, where a passenger was able to claim rights over a bracelet found in a passenger lounge at an airport because the BAB did not manifest the required intention.

Treasure

1.13 All treasure vests in the Crown, therefore it is necessary to determine its definition. The starting point for the modern law is the Treasure Act 1996 ("TA 1996"). Under the Act, treasure is defined as an object which is at least 300 years old when found (s1(1)(a), TA 1996) which is not a coin, but has a precious metal content of 10 per cent by weight (s1(1)(a)(i)) *or* is one of at least two coins (300 years old) in the same find with a 10 per cent weight of precious metal (s1(1)(a)(ii)) *or* is one of at least ten coins (300 years old) in the same find (s1(1)(a)(iii)) *or* an object at least 200 years old (s1(1)(a)(iv)) which belongs to a class designated by the Secretary of State under statutory power in s2(1), TA 1996. Precious metal is taken to mean gold or silver (s3(3), TA 1996). Where treasure is found, it vests in the Crown (s4(1)(b), TA 1996). Under the Act, a person who finds an object which *he believes or has reasonable grounds for believing is treasure* (s8(1)), must notify the coroner within 14 days beginning with the day after the find was made (s8(2)(a)). If later, it is the day on which the finder first believes or has reason to believe the object is treasure (s8(2)(b)). Failure to report is a criminal offence, punishable by three months' imprisonment or a fine (s8(2)(a) and (b)), unless the finder is able to demonstrate a reasonable excuse for failing to notify the coroner (s8(4)). Where the coroner determines the item(s) found constitute treasure, then a reward may be paid (s10(2)).

1.14 As I write this, in February 2019, HM Government has launched public consultation to consider reform of the law on treasure. This is due to an increase in finds which do not fall within the current definition of treasure, because, eg, they are made of base metal, but which might be regarded as 'national treasures' and therefore should be saved. New legislation could be introduced as early as autumn 2019.

Fixtures and Chattels

1.15 One of the most examinable areas is that of fixtures and chattels; a fixture passes as part of the land, a chattel may be taken away. Following the case of **Elitestone Ltd v Morris (1997)(HL)**, it seems clear that there is a **threefold classification** between **chattels, fixtures**, and items which are **part and parcel of the land**. In that case, a building used as a home was standing on brick stilts, but not attached.

Nevertheless, it was 'part and parcel' of the land and had to remain.

1.16 The first stage of assessing whether something is a fixture or a chattel is the Latin maxim *Quidquid Plantatur Solo, Solo Cedit* – That which is attached to the land, becomes part of it. However, this maxim is too crude an instrument and the common law has developed two tests:

(a) **the degree of annexation; and**

(b) **the purpose of annexation.**

(*Holland v Hodgson* (1872)).

(a) Degree of Annexation

1.17 The degree of annexation test states that the more firmly an object is fixed to land or to a building, the more likely it is to be classified as a fixture. Therefore, if something is bolted to the land, the presumption is that it is a fixture; but if it stands under its own weight, it is a chattel.

1.18 Therefore, in **Holland v Hodgson (1872)**, spinning looms bolted to the floor of a factory were held to be fixtures. Likewise, central heating systems, lifts, an alarm system and swimming pool filtration plant were held to be fixtures (**Melluish v BMI (No 3) Ltd (1996)**), and an air conditioning system recessed into the walls of a building was also a fixture (**Aircool Installations v British Telecommunications (1995)**). In contrast, machinery resting on its own weight (**Hulme v Brigham (1943)**), and movable greenhouses (**HE Dibble Ltd v Moore (1970)**), where held to be chattels.

(b) Purpose of Annexation

1.19 The purpose of annexation is the primary test (**Hamp v Bygrave (1983)**) and the one which might rebut the degree of annexation test. The test asks: Is the item fixed for the more convenient use of the item as a chattel, or for the more convenient use of the land? If the former, it's a chattel, even if tightly fixed; if the latter, it's more likely to be a fixture. The purpose of annexation is viewed objectively (**Botham v TSB Bank plc (1997)**).

1.20 Therefore, in **D'Eyncourt v Gregory (1866)**, stone garden ornaments standing under their weight were held to be fixtures because they were part of an architectural design. In **Leigh v Taylor (1902)**, tapestries securely fixed to a wall were held to be chattels because they had to be fixed to be enjoyed, while in **Re Whaley (1908)**, because paintings and tapestries were part of the architectural design of an Elizabethan house, they were held to be fixtures. A further contrast is provided by **Berkley v Poulett (1977)**, where a statue and sundial resting under their weight were held to be chattels; they were there for their aesthetic value, not as part of an overall design.

CHAPTER 2
ESTATES AND INTERESTS IN LAND

Introduction

2.01 This chapter, and the chapter which follows it, are *probably* the most important chapters in this book. The reason is that, between them, they cover the fundamentals of land law: Estate and Interests, and how they are acquired (chapter two) and protection of interests once created (chapter three). These chapters are long, certainly when compared to other chapters in this book, so take some time to learn the material in them, and to understand it, and land law should make a whole lot more sense.

2.02 Now, before I go on, here is the public health warning: Just when you think you have it with land law, it will throw up an exception to the general rule you just understood. So long as you understand when these exceptions to the general rule operate, land law settles down once again and becomes relatively straightforward. With that in mind, let's start by thinking about another fundamental issue which you need to understand: Legal and Equitable rights.

Legal and Equitable Rights

2.03 The estates and interests which we discuss over the coming pages might be **legal** or **equitable**. At its most basic level, **legal rights** were those which were historically recognised by the Courts of Law in England and Wales. However, in England and Wales, we didn't just have Courts of Law, we had Courts of Equity (principally the Court of Chancery) which would recognise other estates and interests. These **estates and interests** could be **similar versions of those recognised in each respective court**, eg, Courts of Law would recognise a legal lease, and Courts of Equity would recognise an equitable lease. These are essentially the same thing, but simply created in slightly different ways. Alternatively, they could recognise entirely different interests: for example, the Courts of Equity would recognise a beneficial ownership under a trust of land, but Courts of Law would not.

2.04 These differences remain today, and the methods of acquiring these interests differ. So, as you read through the following few pages, consider that the estates and interests which exist in English law might be **legal** or **equitable** and whether they are one or the other broadly comes down to how they were created. Now, let's get on with the first part, Estates in Land.

Estates in Land

2.05 Since 1ˢᵗ January 1926, there have been **two estates in land which are capable of being legal**. Note, these estates in land are *capable* of being legal, meaning they could also be equitable.

2.06 These are the **freehold estate** (or to give its formal title, the **fee simple absolute in possession**)(s1(1)(a), LPA 1925) and the **leasehold estate** (its formal title being the **term of years absolute**)(s1(1)(b), LPA 1925).

Not ownership of land – Ownership of title

2.07 The freehold estate is the closest English law comes to awarding ownership of land. The reason for this is that in English law, all land is owned by the Crown, and 'owners' of the land, own not the land, but a period of time in the land. Thus, the freehold estate is a period of ownership of the title to the land, as is the leasehold estate. The fundamental difference between the two is that the freehold estate could go on forever, provided there is someone to inherit the estate, while the leasehold estate will come to an end at the end of the period of the lease. Technically, therefore, I own the title to my house, or my flat, not the land itself.

Freehold Estate

2.08 As indicated, the freehold estate is known technically as the **fee simple absolute in possession**. This definition needs to be broken down to be understood. The **fee** part means that it is inheritable, and the **simple** element means that the inheritance is not limited to a particular individual. The **absolute** element means that the freehold is not subject to any conditions which might bring it, prematurely, to an end. Finally, the **possession** element has it that the current holder of the freehold has the current right to enjoyment of the property associated with the freehold.

2.09 The freehold estate is **capable of being legal**, as stated above. This means that it will **only be legal** if it is *created* **and** *protected* **in the correct way**. This requires the transfer to be **competed by a deed** (s52, LPA 1925). A deed is a document which is **signed by the grantor** (the 'grantor' is the person who executes the deed), **witnessed**, **delivered** (meaning, **dated**), and **states on its face that it is a deed** (s1, Law of Property (Miscellaneous Provisions) Act 1989). If this has been done, it has been *created* in the correct way.

2.10 The second stage is that it must also be *protected* in the correct way. In other words the new title holder must be registered as the new owner of the land under ss4(1) and 27(1), Land Registration Act 2002. Once this is done, the new freeholder was a valid legal freehold estate in land. The issue of protection is discussed in detail in Chapter Three.

2.11 If the freehold title is sold, there is a further stage which needs to be completed, and this is before the deed and registration stages, and that stage is the **contract stage**.

'Contract Stage'

2.12 Generally, contracts have no formalities in English law, which you will know from your study of contract law. However, that is subject to exceptions, and the notable one is in relation to a dealing with land. A contract for the sale of land made on or after 27th September 1989, has to comply with the requirements of s2, Law of Property (Miscellaneous) Provisions Act 1989.

2.13 Section 2, LP(MP)A 1989 applies requires that a valid contract for the sale of land must be:

      (i)   in writing;

      (ii)   contain all the terms; AND,

      (iii) be signed by both parties

2.14 The requirement of writing speaks for itself. The document may be a single document containing all the terms which is signed by both parties, or it may be two identical documents which are signed, then exchanged by, both parties.

2.15 A document which proposes to vary the terms as originally agreed must comply with s2 (**McCausland v Duncan Lawrie Ltd (1996)**), but the document itself may incorporate its terms by reference to another document (s2(2)).

2.16 When it comes to the signature, it would usually be the recognised hand-written signature of the parties, but the recent case of **Neocleous v Rees (2019)** permitted the automatic footer 'signature' at the end of an email to count as signature for the purposes of a section 2 contract. While this decision is only a County Court decision, it does demonstrate a clear movement towards electronic creation and execution of land documentation.

2.17 Though the previous discussion relates to contracts for the sale of land, s2, LP(MP)A 1989 also needs to be satisfied in other situations, eg, options to purchase, rights of pre-emption, etc. These are highlighted and discussed later. Note, also, that s2 does not apply in some other scenarios, eg, purchase of land at public auction, or to situations where an implied trust arises (s2(5), LP(MP)A 1989).

Leasehold Estate

2.18 This is the other estate in land. It's technical name is the **term of years absolute**. Though a lease may be for a term (period) of years, eg, 999 years, it may equally be for a period of less than a year, eg, a leasehold estate could be for six months (s205(1)(xxvi), LPA 1925).

2.19 In order to be a valid leasehold estate, the interest claimed must have the **characteristics of a lease**. In **Street v Mountford (1985)(HL)**, it was said that a lease has three characteristics. First, it must have a **certain term**; secondly, it must give the tenant **exclusive possession**; and, thirdly, it must charge a **rent**. However, s205(1)(xxvii), LPA 1925 does not list rent as a requirement, which was taken .to be the position in **Ashburn Anstalt v Arnold (1989)(CA)**. However, most leases would require the payment of rent.

Certain term

2.20 A lease must be for a fixed period of time, having a certain start date and a certain end date. Thus, a lease for the 'length of the war' was not valid (**Lace v Chantler (1944)**), nor one for a period until the land was needed by the landlord for development purposes (**Prudential Assurance Co Ltd v London Residuary Body (1992)**).

2.21 Where the term is not set at the start of the tenancy, this may be valid as a lease on a **periodic tenancy** basis. That is, if payment of rent is monthly, then it will be a **monthly periodic tenancy**, or paid annually, then an **annual periodic tenancy** (**Prudential Assurance Co Ltd v London Residuary Body (1992)**). Both would be valid because they have a certain term, ie, the period for whatever the rent is paid.

Exclusive possession

2.22 A tenant must have exclusion possession of the property. This means the right to exclude others from the property, including the landlord.

2.23 Where a claimed leasehold estate does not have the characteristics of a lease, then it will not be a lease, but may be something else. For example, it may be a **licence**. A licence is a **mere permission** to be on the land but **it is not a property right**.

Leasehold Estate: Capable of being legal

2.24 This is an estate in land which is capable of being legal. Again, it is only *capable* of being legal, meaning if it is not *created* and *protected* in the correct way, it will not be legal, but may be equitable.

2.25 Every lease of **more than three years** must be **created by deed** (s52, LPA 1925; s1, LP(MP)A 1989). Whether it is *protected* in the correct way will depend on the length of the lease. If it **is lease of more than seven years**, it must be **substantively registered** (s27(2)(b)(i) Land Registration Act 2002). If the lease is **more than three years, but less than seven years**, then such leases are **protected automatically** without the need for registration because they are said to override under sch3, para1, LRA 2002 because they are for a **term not exceeding seven years**. This means they would automatically bind a new owner of the freehold title. This is discussed in more detail in Chapter Three.

2.26 Earlier, it was mentioned that in some circumstances land law creates exceptions to its general rule. Well, here is the first one. A legal lease can be created informally, ie, without a deed, so long as it is **not longer than three years**, takes effect **in possession**, and for 'best' rent, ie, market rent, without payment of a premium (s54(2), LPA 1925). This is a legal lease, even though there is no deed, and it is protected because it overrides under sch3, para 1, LRA 2002, as explained in 2.25, above.

2.27 If the lease is not created or protected in the correct way, then it may be a **legal period tenancy**, if it complies with s54(2), LPA 1925, or, as is also possible, an **equitable lease**.

Equitable Lease

2.28 An equitable lease can arise in a number of ways. First, as stated, it can arise because an attempted legal lease fails; secondly, only a s2, LP(MP)A 1989 agreement to create a lease has been agreed; or, thirdly, the person granting the lease has only an equitable lease themselves, so can only grant an equitable lease. In the first and second situations, so long as the document complies with s2, LP(MP)A 1989, see paras 2.13 – 2.17, above, it will be a valid equitable lease. In the third situation, it only needs to have signed writing to be valid (s53(1)(a), LPA 1925). This different statutory requirement in the third scenario is reflected in the fact that the lease can only have been equitable from the outset.

2.29 An equitable lease is protected in registered title by a **notice on the Charges Register** of the registered freehold (s32, LRA 2002). Where the freehold title is unregistered, then the equitable leaseholder protects their interest by registering a C(iv) land charge (s2(4), Land Charges Act 1972). This is discussed in more detail in Chapter Three.

Legal Interests in Land

2.30 We have looked at the estates in land, but land law is about more than the estates. Land cannot be used as well as it might be without a whole range of other, lesser, interests. These interests are many and varied, and, like estates in land, they can be **legal** or **equitable**. Let's start with those interests which are capable **of being legal**. There are three which are important for our purposes, so they are mentioned; the others are of only minor significance.

2.31 The interests in land which are capable of being legal are contained in s1(2), LPA 1925. These are **easements and profits** (s1(2)(a), LPA 1925). An easement is the right enjoyed over your neighbour's land, eg, a right of way over your neighbour's land. A profit is the right to take something from another's land, eg, firewood from woodland on someone else's land. Easements are an important interest in land and discussed in detail in Chapter Five.

2.32 A **charge by way of legal mortgage** (s1(2)(c), LPA 1925) is a **mortgage** in plain language, and that is a loan of money secured by a charge over the borrower's property. This is an incredibly important interest in land and is discussed in more detail in Chapter Six.

2.33 Finally, a **landlord's right of entry** (s1(2)(e), LPA 1925), which allows the landlord to enter to terminate a lease, or enter to enforce a rent charge. These are discussed in more detail in Chapter 11.

2.34 In order for these interests to be legal, they must be created and protected in the correct way. First, they must satisfy the requirements of the provision. For example, an **easement**, to be **legal**, must be for the **length of a freehold or a leasehold estate** (s1(2)(a), LPA 1925). Secondly, it must then be created by **deed**, see para 2.09, above. Thirdly, and finally, the interest may need to be registered to be protected. As the particular interests are protected in different ways, you should look at the relevant part of the chapters where that interest is discussed in detail in this book.

2.35 Once again, if the conditions are not met in some way, then the interest **will not be legal**, but it *may* **be equitable**.

Equitable Interests in Land

2.36 All other interests not listed in s1(2), LPA 1925 will be equitable (s1(3), LPA 1925). The most common equitable interests are **restrictive covenants** (Chapter Four), **beneficial interests under a trust** (Chapters Eight and Nine), and **Estate Contracts**. It is worth saying a little more about estate contracts.

2.37 An estate contract is an equitable interest in land. It is, in essence, a contractual right and includes important rights such as **options to purchase** and **rights of pre-emption**. An **option to purchase** is the **right to purchase at the option of the buyer**; a **right of pre-emption** is the **right**

to first refusal once the seller decides to sell.

2.38 The **contract stage of a land contract** is also an **estate contract**. Equity will give the remedy of specific performance once the contract stage is met because of the maxim **equity looks on as done that which ought to be done**. This means that the seller will have to execute a deed to transfer legal title. The estate contract under a land purchase contract may be protected by registration as a notice in the Charges Register where title to the estate is registered (s32, LRA 2002), or as a C(iv) land charge where title to the estate is unregistered (s2(4)(iv), LCA 1972). This is discussed in more detail in Chapter Three.

2.39 The formalities for the creation of an equitable interest are, generally speaking, dependant on the **type of equitable interest**. As indicated, **estate contracts** need to comply with **s2, LP(MP)A 1989**, whereas interests such as **equitable easements** and **restrictive covenants**, need only comply with **s53(1)(a), LPA 1925 (signed writing)**. A **beneficial interest under a trust which is expressly created** must comply with **s53(1)(b), LPA 1925**, meaning that it must be **evidenced by signed writing**, whereas a **beneficial interest under an implied trust** is **not subject to formalities (s53(2), LPA 1925)**. This is discussed in detail in chapter nine.

CHAPTER 3
REGISTERED AND UNREGISTERED TITLE

REGISTERED TITLE: Introduction

3.01 Since the nineteenth century, there have been many attempts to create a comprehensive register of all land ownership in England and Wales. The latest attempt at completing the process is to be found in the Land Registration Act 2002 ('LRA 2002') which replaces the Land Registration Act 1925, though some of the old case law remains relevant. Registration aims to simplify land transfers by requiring all interests in land to be on one central register which is open to all. However, the reality is much less true.

Rationale of Registration

3.02 A system of registration of title where all ownership interests are provided in one place, accessible to the public, makes good sense for a number of reasons. First, it provides external evidence of ownership and limits the chances of loss occurring because of the loss of key documents. Secondly, it allows land to be bought and sold more easily, without the need to investigate ownership interests over lengthy and sustained periods.

Three Principles of Registered Title

3.03 There are said to be three principles behind registration of title:

(i) The Mirror Principle – This is the idea that the register should *reflect*, fully, all the interests which exist in respect of title to land.

(ii) The Curtain Principle – This is intended as a rather

16

loose metaphor. The law allows a purchaser not to worry about beneficial interests which might exist in a trust of land by drawing a curtain over them. However, the purchaser must pay the 'capital' monies to at least two people or to a trust corporation.

(iii) The Insurance principle – This is the idea that the state guarantees the accuracy of the register and it will compensate the purchaser for losses which occur as a result of the register being inaccurate.

Format of the Register

3.04 The register is not one register, but it is split into three registers:

(i) Property Register – This register describes the land by reference to a plan and outlines the rights which benefit the land.

(ii) Proprietorship Register – This register provides the name and address of the proprietor (the owner), the nature of the title (ie, whether it is freehold or leasehold), and whether there are any restrictions affecting the owner's ability to deal with the property.

(iii) Charges Register – This register lists the rights which burden the land, eg, restrictive covenants, etc.

What attracts protection on the register?

3.05 There are three categories of registerable interests:

(i) Registered Estates – There are two estates which are to be registered: (a) Fee simple absolute in possession (freehold); and, (b) Term of Years Absolute of more than seven years (leasehold).

(ii) Registered Charges – mortgages.

(iii) Other Registerable Interests – Restrictive Covenants; (some) Easements; Options to Purchase; and, a Spousal Right of Occupation. Under s32, LRA 2002, these should be protected by entry as a Notice on the Charges Register of the burdened estate. Failure to register an interest gives rise to a loss of priority with the result that it will not bind a purchaser.

Restrictions on the Proprietorship Register

3.06 Sometimes there will be some restriction or limitation on the owner's ability to deal freely with their property (s40, LRA 2002). These limitations will be registered literally as a 'restriction' on the Proprietorship Register. The classic example is requirement that in order to defeat a beneficial interest under a trust of land, the 'capital' monies should be paid to two trustees or a trust corporation. This is known as overreaching and is explained at the end of this chapter. A restriction may be indefinite, for a fixed period, or until the occurrence of an event. A restriction operates as a 'warning light' to a potential purchaser.

Notices on the Charges Register

3.07 Most interests, as indicated, will be protected by this method. Notices might either be unilateral or agreed, but in any event the holder of the benefit must register the notice against the title of the burdened land. Failure to register an interest by notice when it ought to have been causes the holder of the interest to suffer a loss of priority against a purchaser for valuable consideration (s29, LRA 2002). Note, entry of a notice does not mean the interest is valid; that is a separate question of law. Registration is only concerned with protection.

3.08 Some interests cannot be protected by notice. These include, interests under a trust of land (s33(a), LRA 2002), a lease of three years or less (s33(b), LRA 2002) and, a covenant agreed between a landlord and tenant (s33(c), LRA 2002).

Interests which Override

3.09 The idea behind title registration is to ensure a complete and accurate register of all interests in or over land. However, there is one significant exception to this under the LRA 2002, namely interests which override. These are interests which *may be* binding on a purchaser, yet do not appear on the register. Hayton (1981) described them as a 'crack in the mirror'. Under the LRA 2002 it is envisaged that the list of interests which override will be reduced. The key interests which override are: (i) leases of seven years or less; (ii) interests which override by actual occupation; (iii) implied legal easements.

(i)   Leases of seven years or less

3.10 Where the lease is a legal lease for a term of seven years or less, it will override under sch 3, para 1, Land Registration Act 2002. Remember, leases of more than seven years must be substantively registered.

(ii)   Interests of those in actual occupation

3.11 This is the most significant of all the overriding interests. The law is contained in sch 3, para 2, Land Registration Act 2002. First, the person must have an interest (actual occupation is not a right in itself) and protect it by being in actual occupation of the land.

'an interest'

3.12 First, the interest must be a property right, and a mere licence will not satisfy this requirement (**Strand Securities v Caswell (1965)**). Interests which might be protected under sch 3, para 2, LRA 2002:

- Beneficial interests under a trust (**William's & Glyn's Bank v Boland (1981)**), unless the interest is overreached;

- Equitable leases (**Grace Rymer Investments Ltd v Waite (1958)**);

- Estate contracts (**Bridges v Mees (1957)**);

- Options to purchase (**Ferrishurst Ltd v Wallcite Ltd (1999)**) / rights of pre-emption (**Kling v Keston Properties Ltd (1983)**).

'actual occupation'

3.13 Once the claimant has identified an interest, they must demonstrate that they were also in actual occupation in order to protect the interest. Actual occupation is a question of fact, but there must be "some degree of permanence and continuity" (*per* Lord Oliver in **Abbey National v Cann (1991)**). It is not possible to occupy through a third party (**Strand Securities v Caswell (1965)**), unless they are a caretaker, ie, in a formal employment role, though some temporary absence from the property, eg, for a holiday or hospital treatment, will not break the continuity of the occupation (**Chhokar v Chhokar (1984)**). Where an individual claims an interest in the whole of a piece of land, but is in actual occupation of only part of it, then the interest will only override for that part of the land.

3.14 However, the purchaser will not be bound by an overriding interests where (a) the interest is not disclosed on reasonable inquiry; or (ii) it belongs to a person whose occupation would not have been obvious on a reasonable inspection of the land.

3.15 A spousal right of occupation will not override by actual occupation (s30(10)(b), Family Law Act 1996).

(iii) Implied legal easements

3.16 Implied legal easements override by sch 3, para 3, Land Registration Act 2002. Express legal easements and all equitable easements must be registered. This is discussed in detail in chapter five.

UNREGISTERED TITLE: Introduction

3.17 While there is a desire to have all ownership of land recorded in a single register title to some land in England and Wales remains '**unregistered**'. This means that ownership is not recorded in a single register, but must be investigated by different means. However, there is one important point to note, namely, that though we are concerned with unregistered title, there is, in fact, a **limited scheme of registration of interests**.

Legal and Equitable Interests

3.18 In unregistered title, **legal interests** are binding on a purchaser without the need for registration because *legal interests bind the whole world*. Insofar as **equitable interests** are concerned, these fall into three categories:

    (i)   equitable interests which must be registered (Land Charges Act (LCA) 1972);

    (ii)   equitable interests subject to overreaching, eg, interests under a trust of land;

    (iii) equitable interests not in (a) and (b), subject to the doctrine of notice.

3.19 However, there is one legal interest which does have to be registered, namely a **puisne mortgage**. This is a class C(i) land charge.

(a) equitable interests which must be registered (Land Charges Act (LCA) 1972)

3.20 Under the Land Charges Act 1972, certain interests will only be protected if they are registered. Once registered, the interest is binding on a purchaser; if not registered, the interest will be **void** against a purchaser depending on the *type of purchaser*. The LCA 1972 envisages two types of purchaser: (i) a **purchaser for valuable consideration** (which includes marriage consideration) and (ii) a **purchaser for money or money's worth** (which is something which might be quantified in monetary terms so excludes marriage consideration).

3.21 Under the limited scheme of registration, there are six classes of interest: Class A, B, C, D, E and F. The main interests will be considered.

Class C (iv) land charge – estate contract

3.22 Under s2(4)(iv), LCA 1972 estate contracts should be registered as a class C (iv) land charge. Examples of an estate contract include an option to purchase, or a right of pre-emption, etc. Failure to register this land charge renders the interest **void against a purchaser of the *legal* estate for money or money's worth** (s4(6), LCA 1972).

Class D (ii) land charge – restrictive covenant

3.23 A restrictive covenant is an agreement to limit the use of land, eg, not to build an extension. This interest is an equitable interest. Failure to register this land charge renders the interest **void against a purchaser of the *legal* estate for money or money's worth** (s4(6), LCA 1972). Covenants created before 1st January 1926 are still governed by the doctrine of notice. These are still relevant, so it is worth bearing this in mind.

Class D (iii) land charge – equitable easements

3.24 An equitable easement is one which has not been created by deed, or is not for the length of either of the legal estates in land. Failure to register this land charge renders the interest **void against a purchaser of the *legal* estate for money or money's worth** (s4(6), LCA 1972). As with restrictive covenants, this only relates to equitable easements created since 1st January 1926. Equitable easements created earlier are still subject to the doctrine of notice.

Class F land charge – Family Law Act 1996

3.25 This is a right of occupation available to a spouse whose name is not on the legal title. This is not an interest in land, rather a mere statutory right of occupation. Failure to register this land charge renders it void against a **purchaser of *any* interest** for **valuable consideration** (s4(5) and (8), LCA 1972).

(b) equitable interests subject to overreaching, eg, interests under a trust of land

3.26 Overreaching is the process by which an interest is land is removed and turned into an interest in the purchase money paid by the buyer of the land. For overreaching to occur, the purchase monies must be paid to two trustees or a trust corporation. This is concerned with interests which are quantifiable in monetary terms, eg, an interest under a trust of land.

(c) equitable interests not in (a) and (b), subject to the doctrine of notice

3.27 Those interests not in (a) and (b) are dependent for their enforceability on the **doctrine of notice**. These are:

(i)   Interests excluded by the LCA 1972, ie, pre-1926 equitable easements and restrictive covenants, and covenants between landlord and tenant.

(ii) A beneficial interest under a trust overreaching has not occurred.

(iii) Mere equities.

(iv) Interests arising by estoppel.

3.28 If a purchaser wishes to take a property free of any equitable interests, then he must demonstrate that he is a bona fide purchaser for value of a legal estate without notice: This is the essence of the **doctrine of notice**. This means that he must be a good faith purchaser of the legal estate providing valuable consideration (including marriage consideration) without notice of the equitable interest. There are three types of notice:

(i)   **Actual notice** – where the purchaser has actual knowledge of a third party interest (s198(1), LPA 1925);

(ii)   **Constructive notice** – where the purchaser can be taken to know of the existence of an interest, but does not ask questions which mean they would obtain further information about the interest;

(iii) **Imputed notice** – this is notice obtained by the purchaser's agent, eg, a solicitor during the course of the purchase (s199(1)(ii)(b), LPA 1925).

Overreaching

3.29 This concept scares most students of land law, but is actually a very simple idea. When purchasing property, the purchaser would be better advised that land free of equitable interests under a trust will be more valuable. Therefore, he will want to ensure that when purchasing property, the purchase rids the land of any equitable interest under a trust – this is done by the **process of overreaching**. Overreaching takes the equitable interest off the land and transfers it into an equitable interest in the purchase money paid by the purchaser. This balances the interests of a purchaser who will wish to take the land free of equitable interests under a trust, and the person with the interest who at least receives monetary compensation in the form of the purchase price.

3.30 The statutory provisions which relate to overreaching are ss2 and 27, Law of Property Act 1925. This stipulates that overreaching occurs where the conveyance (payment of purchase monies, or payment of mortgage monies) is made to at least two trustees or to a trust corporation.

3.31 The two leading cases on overreaching are **Williams & Glyn's Bank Ltd v Boland (1981)** and **City of London Building Society v Flegg (1988)**.

3.32 In *Boland*, a wife contributed to the purchase price of the property, but the property was registered in the husband's name alone. So, even though not the registered legal owner, the wife had an equitable interest under a presumed resulting trust (**Bull v Bull (1955)**). Subsequently, the husband mortgaged the property to the claimant bank, and failed to maintain the repayments. The question arose as to whether the bank was bound by the wife's equitable interest. It was held that a mortgage was a qualifying conveyance for the purposes of overreaching, but that in failing to pay the mortgage monies to two trustees, the bank took the house subject to the wife's interest as a person with an interest in actual occupation.

3.33 In contrast, in *Flegg*, parents, a daughter and son-in-law purchased a house together. The parents provided half the purchase price, but the house was registered in the joint names of the daughter and son-in-law. Some time later, the daughter and son-in-law mortgaged the property to the City of London Building Society. When they defaulted on the loan, the issue of the rights of the parties arose. The parents claimed an overriding interest in actual occupation under s70(1)(g), LRA 1925. However, the building society successfully argued that as the mortgage monies had been paid to two persons under s2, LPA 1925, the interests of the parents had been overreached and the building society took the property free of their interest.

3.34 It is important to note that **overreaching operates in the same way** whether title to the land is unregistered or registered.

CHAPTER 4
FREEHOLD COVENANTS

Introduction

4.01 In English law, freehold owners may agree with another to do, or not to do, something in relation to their land. Such agreements are known as **covenants**. A covenant to do something, eg, to maintain a boundary fence, is a **positive covenant**; a covenant not to do something, eg, not to use a property for business purposes, is a **restrictive (or, negative) covenant**.

4.02 When the original parties agree to something, all covenants agreed between them are enforceable, whether they are positive or negative. However, problems start in English law when the land subject to the covenant is sold to a new owner and the question arises as to **whether covenants can be enforce by, or against, a new owner**. Here, we look at questions of the rules at **common law** and the rules in **equity**, since both treat covenants differently. However, before we start on that, it's useful to understand the terminology.

Terminology

4.03 A covenant is a **promise contained in a deed**. The parties to the covenant are known as the **covenantor** and the **covenantee**. The party who **makes the promise** is the **covenantor**; the party who receives the promise, ie, **takes its benefit**, is the **covenantee**. The **burdened land**, ie, the land of the covenantor, is sometimes referred to as the **servient land**; the land which has the **benefit**, ie, the land of the covenantee, is sometimes referred to as the **dominant land**.

Original parties

4.04 Now, as already stated, the original parties can agree to any covenants, positive or negative, and they will be enforceable between them as a matter of contract. Problems start when the original covenantor sells their land and this raises a question: **Can the new owner of the burdened land have the covenants enforced against them?** Also, when the original covenantee sells their land, this raises the question: **Can the new owner of the dominant land enforce the covenants against the current owner of the burdened land?**

4.05 Well, it sounds a bit complex, but the *basic* position can actually be summed up in two sentences:

At common law, the burden of a covenant will not pass to a new owner of the burdened land

In Equity, the burden of a covenant may pass to a new owner of the burdened land, provided the covenant is restrictive (negative)

4.06 That is the general position. However, as you know from studying law, matters are rarely that straightforward. The common law rule is subject to exceptions, and both common law and equity are subject to conditions which must be satisfied. We'll start our discussion by looking at the common law position.

Common Law (Benefit)

Will the benefit of a covenant pass to a new owner of the dominant land at common law?

4.07 The short answer to this question is 'Yes', provided it is by one of the following methods: (i) Express Assignment; (ii) the conditions from **P&A Swift Investment v Combined English**

Stores (1989) have been met; (iii) Contract (Rights of Third Parties) Act 1999; (iv) s56, Law of Property Act 1925.

(i) Express Assignment

4.08 Under s136, Law of Property Act 1925, for the benefit of the covenant to pass at common law, written notice of the assignment should be given to the covenantor, ie, the party with the burden.

(ii) Conditions from P&A Swift Investment v Combined English Stores (1989)

4.09 The conditions from *P&A Swift* are that:

(i)   Covenant must touch and concern the land;

(ii) The parties must intend the benefit to pass;

(iii) Successor in title to covenantee must hold a legal estate; AND,

(iv) Original covenantee must have held a legal estate.

4.10 A covenant will **touch and concern the land** if it is for the benefit of the dominant land, affecting its **nature, quality, mode of use, or value**. Thus anything expressed to be personal is not likely to satisfy this condition. For the parties to **intend the benefit to pass** they could use **express words**, or rely on the **implication** under **s78, Law of Property Act 1925**, which deems a covenant to be made with the covenantee and those who obtain the land from him.

4.11 The requirement that the **successor in title to covenantee must hold a legal estate** is almost self-explanatory. The legal estates in land are those listed in **s1(1), Law of Property Act 1925**. The benefit will not pass where the covenantee has only an equitable interest in the dominant land. The final condition, namely that the **original covenantee must have held a legal estate**, is also rather straightforward. Note, the legal estate held does not have to be the same one (**Smith and Snipes Hall Farm Ltd v River Douglas Catchment Board (1949)**).

(iii) Contract (Rights of Third Parties) Act 1999

4.12 The 1999 Act requires a term in the agreement to give a third party some right of action, or to confer a benefit upon them. This is of limited significance.

(iv) s56, Law of Property Act 1925

4.13 This provision states that an individual may benefit from a covenant, even though not named in the conveyance.

Common Law (Burden)

Will the burden of a covenant pass to a new owner of the servient land at common law?

4.14 The general rule is that the **burden of a covenant will NOT pass at common law (Austerberry v Oldham Corporation (1885)(CA); Rhone v Stephens (1994)(HL)**). The original covenantor remains liable (**s79, Law of Property Act 1925**), but only for damages (**Tophams Ltd v Earl of Sefton (1967)**). However, there are some useful exceptions which you should know: (i) the 'chain of indemnity' covenants; (ii) the rule in Halsall v Brizell.

(i) 'chain of indemnity' covenants

4.15 Each time the burdened land is sold, an indemnity covenant is obtained from the buyer for the benefit of the seller. This indemnity has the effect that if the original covenantor is sued for the buyer's breach of covenant, the buyer agrees to indemnify the seller, ie, pay the seller's damages.

4.16 However, an indemnity must be obtained each time the burdened land is sold so that a 'chain' of indemnity covenants is created. Problematically, if on one conveyance the indemnity covenant is forgotten, the chain is broken; **the chain is only as strong as its weakest link**. The chain can also be broken by insolvency or unavailability of the party which agreed it.

4.17 Even where the chain is complete, enforcement is indirect and means that damages are passed down the 'chain'. The remedy the covenantee or their successor would usually want, eg, an injunction, is not available to them.

(ii) the rule in Halsall v Brizell

4.18 This is sometimes known as the rule of **mutual benefit and burden**. One party cannot deny they are subject to a burden if they also enjoy a benefit. A common example would be an obligation for one party to make a financial contribution to the maintenance of an access road which they use to access their land; they have the benefit of use of the road, so they should pay towards its maintenance. The rule has its origins in **Halsall v Brizell (1957)**, but has developed since that decision.

4.19 The modern expression of the conditions for the 'rule in Halsall v Brizell' come from **Davies v Jones (2009)(CA)**:

   (1)   The benefit and burden must be conferred in the same transaction;

   (2)   The benefit and the burden must be linked in some way, as in the example provided in para 4.18, above. Whether this link is satisfied will often be a question of construction of the documents conferring the benefit and imposing the burden (**Wilkinson v Kerdene (2013)(CA)**);

   (3)   The individual subject to the burden must have the

freedom to reject it, and thereby not be able to enjoy the benefit (**Thamesmead Town Ltd v Allotey (1998)**).

Equity (Burden)

Will the burden of a covenant pass to a new owner of the servient land in equity?

4.20 We will now consider the rules in equity, but we will start with the burden. The reason for this is that if the burden does not pass, there is no reason to consider the benefit in equity.

4.21 For the burden of a covenant to pass in equity, the following conditions must be satisfied:

(i)   The covenant must be negative in substance;

(ii) The covenant must accommodate the dominant tenement;

(iii) The original parties must have intended that the burden should bind successors;

(iv) The person against whom the covenant is being enforced must have notice of it.

(i)   The covenant must be negative in substance

4.22 The covenant must be negative in substance, even if the language sounds positive. Therefore, a covenant to maintain land as an open space, free of buildings, is negative in substance because it limits the erection of buildings, even though the language is positive (**Tulk v Moxhay (1848)**). The reason for this restriction is that equity will not require someone to carry out an act which involves spending money – putting their hand in their pocket (**Haywood v Brunswick Building Society (1881)**).

4.23 A covenant which is mixed, ie, partly positive and partly negative, may be severed and the negative part upheld (**Shepherd Homes Ltd v Sandham (No 2) (1971)**).

(ii)   The covenant must accommodate the dominant tenement

4.24 The covenant must be for the benefit of the land, not merely of benefit to the owner. Here, reliance is placed on **P & A Swift Investments v Combined English Stores (1989)** and whether the covenant touches and concerns the land, meaning the covenant affects the nature, quality, mode of use, or value, of the land.

(iii)   The original parties must have intended that the burden should bind successors

4.25 The original parties could have intended the burden should bind either by the use of express wording in the original conveyance, or place reliance on the implied intention under s79, Law of Property Act 1925. However, the statutory provision may not be relied upon where a contrary intention is expressed (**Morrells of Oxford Ltd v Oxford United FC (2000)**).

(iv)   The person against whom the covenant is being enforced must have notice of it

4.26 Whether the correct notice provisions apply depends on whether title to the land is registered or unregistered. Where **title is unregistered**, they should be protected by a class D(ii) land charge and, where registered, this constitutes notice (s198, LPA 1925). If it is not registered, a purchaser of the legal estate is not bound (s4(6), Land Charges Act 1972). For covenants agreed before 1st January 1926, the doctrine of notice continues to apply.

4.27 Where **title is registered**, a notice should be entered on the Charges Register of the burdened land (s32, LRA 2002). If not registered, the purchaser of the legal estate is not bound (s29, LRA 2002).

Equity (Benefit)

Will the benefit of a covenant pass to a new owner of the dominant land in equity?

4.28 The answer to this question is 'Yes', provided the following are satisfied:

> (i) The covenant touches and concerns the land; AND,
>
> (ii) The covenant has been either (a) Annexed to the land; (b) Assigned to the covenantee's successor; or, (c) there is a building scheme in place.

(i)   The covenant touches and concerns the land

4.29 Whether a covenant is for the benefit of the land will be determined, once again, by **P & A Swift Investments v Combined English Stores (1989)** and asking whether the covenant affects the **nature, quality, mode of use, or value**, of the land.

(ii)(a) Annexation

4.30 Annexation means 'attaching' the benefit of the covenant to the land. This can be done by express words or by the statutory wording in **s78, LPA 1925**.

(ii)(b) Assignment

4.31 This is the process of transferring the benefit to the new covenantee every time the dominant land is sold. Note: The benefit must be assigned each time (**Miles v Easter (1933)**).

(iii)(c) Building Scheme

4.32 The final method is by a building scheme. The criteria for this were set down in **Elliston v Reacher (1908)**. They are:

> (i)   All purchasers acquire their property from the same (common) seller;
>
> (ii) Before sale, the seller has divided the estate into plots;
>
> (iii) Any restrictive covenants were intended by the seller to continue to benefit the plots;
>
> (iv) Each buyer purchases a plot understanding that the covenants benefit all the other plots in the scheme.

4.33 The criteria under 'building schemes' are difficult to meet.

Reform

4.34 As can be seen, the law in this area is a complex of rules and conditions which must be satisfied. With this in mind, there has been an agenda for reform for a number of years. In 2011, the Law Commission published a report, 'Easements, Covenants and Profits à Prendre' (Law Com No327), with a Bill annexed for reform of the law.

4.35 The principal reforms recommended to the law on covenants involve simplification of the law of restrictive covenants, making life easier for buyers of land, and allowing for the benefit and burden of positive obligations to be enforced by, and against, owners of the dominant and servient land. This would replace the covenant with a generic 'land obligation' label.

CHAPTER 5
EASEMENTS AND PROFITS

Introduction

5.01 An easement is a property right enjoyed against another's land. Most easements are **positive**, ie, allowing the holder of the easement to do something on the neighbour's land, eg, an easement of way across your neighbour's land. However, easements might also be **negative**, which effectively restricts your neighbour's use of their land. A good example would be an easement of light which restricts your neighbour from building on their land in any way which might restrict the light to your land. With negative easements there is, of course, an overlap with restrictive covenants (see chapter four), which is why the law is careful not to recognise negative easements (**Phipps v Pears (1964)**).

5.02 To determine whether a right which is claimed is a valid easement: First, it must have the **characteristics of an easement**; secondly, it must have been **acquired as an easement**; thirdly, it must have been **protected in the correct way**. This chapter will follow this order.

Characteristics of Easements

5.03 For an interest claimed to have the characteristics of an easement, it needs to satisfy the criteria from **Re Ellenbrough Park (1956)**, confirmed by the recent Supreme Court case of **Regency Villas Ltd v Diamond Resorts Ltd (2018)**. They are:

> (i)   There must be a dominant and a servient tenement;
>
> (ii) The right must accommodate the dominant tenement;

(iii)   The dominant and servient tenements must be owned or occupied by different people;

(iv)   The interest must lie in grant.

5.04 While these are the principal criteria, there are other factors which also need to be considered: (v) No expenditure by servient tenement; (vi) Is it recreational?; (vii) May not be exclusive possession.

(i)   There must be a dominant and a servient tenement

5.05 For every right which purports to be an easement, there must be a dominant tenement to enjoy the right, and a servient tenement over which the right is exercised. 'Tenement' simply means 'land' in this context; so, there must be dominant and servient land.

5.06 It is often said that an easement cannot exist 'in gross', ie, separate from dominant land which can enjoy it.

5.07 This requirement is satisfied in most cases.

(ii)   The right must accommodate the dominant tenement

5.08 The right must be for the benefit of the dominant tenement. It must not be for mere personal advantage as this will not be an easement. In **Hill v Tupper (1863)**, a canal company leased land adjoining a canal to Hill giving him the exclusive right to let out pleasure boats on the canal. Tupper, an inn-keeper who owned premises abutting the canal began to let his own boats on the canal. Hill sued Tupper for interference with his alleged easement. The court held that Hill's right was personal, a licence, and that Tupper's action was not an interference with a property right. Hill did not have an easement, so could not sue Tupper for interference with it.

5.09 Though the land must accommodate the dominant tenement, it does not have to be next to the servient tenement (**Pugh v Savage (1970)**), so long as it is sufficiently close to the dominant tenement to provide a practical benefit to it. Thus, it might be said that there cannot be an easement over land in Northumberland for the benefit of land in Kent.

(iii) The dominant and servient tenements must be owned or occupied by different people

5.10 Since an easement is a right one enjoys over another's land, it stands to reason that the lands in question must be owned or occupied by different persons. The stipulation that the land be owned *or occupied* means that landlord and tenant relationships do not infringe the characteristic. For example, Bob owns Whiteacre and Greenacre; they are adjoining properties. Bob leases Greenacre to Clara. Some while later, Bob grants Clara an easement across Whiteacre so Clara can store items in a shed on Whiteacre. This could be a valid easement, even though Bob is clearly the freehold owner of both Whiteacre and Greenacre, but importantly, Clara is the leaseholder of Greenacre.

(iv) The interest must lie in grant

5.11 The easement must be a right which is capable of being granted by a grantor (party giving the easement) to a grantee (party receiving the easement). This simplistic statement has more to it. First, there must be a capable grantor and grantee, meaning the parties are of full age and sound mind, and that the grantor is in possession of an estate in the servient tenement, and that the grantee is in possession of an estate in the dominant tenement. Secondly, the right must be something which is capable of being granted by deed. Thirdly, and linked to the previous point, the right must be sufficiently definite or, in other words, in the general nature of rights capable of being recognised as easements.

5.12 Thus, rights which have been sufficiently well-defined to satisfy the fourth condition include: the right to affix a board advertising a public house to a neighbouring house (**Moody v Steggles (1879)**); the right to use a toilet on another's land

(**Miller v Emcer Products Ltd (1956)**); a right to store coal in a neighbour's shed (**Wright v Macadam (1949)**). Conversely, those rights which are not sufficiently defined and consequently have been held incapable of amounting to easements include: the right to a view (**Aldred's Case (1610)**); a right to privacy (**Browne v Flower (1911)**); a right to receive a television signal (**Hunter v Canary Wharf Limited (1997)**).

5.13 Those are the criteria from Re Ellenbrough Park, but as stated at paragraph 5.04, above, there are other matters which the courts also take into consideration when assessing whether an interest claimed has the characteristics of an easement.

(v) No expenditure by servient tenement

5.14 Generally, the servient owner should not be required to spend money (**Duke of Westminster v Guild (1985)**). The role of the servient owner is passive in that they merely allow the dominant owner to exercise their right without interference. Therefore, an interest claimed which requires the servient owner to undertake positive acts is not, generally, characteristic of an easement.

5.15 There are, however, exceptions. For example, maintenance of a boundary fence has been upheld as a valid easement, even though it would involve the servient owner spending money (**Crow v Wood (1971)**). In the recent case of **Churston Golf Club Ltd v Haddock (2019)**, the CA declined to interpret what was clearly a positive covenant as an easement of fencing because the wording of the provision did not support that interpretation. This reversed the High Court decision in the case. Thus, it seems that for an easement of fencing to be found, the language must be clear in expressing what it is creates.

5.16 In **Regency Villas Ltd v Diamond Resorts Ltd (2018)**, the SC held that owners of timeshare properties could benefit from valid easements to use sporting facilities and gardens surrounding the property. This was so notwithstanding running costs and operational responsibilities imposed on the servient owner by the easement.

(vi) Is it recreational?

5.17 Historically, the law was troubled by recreational easements because they were not typical of the sort of easements which might be valid. However, the recent case of **Regency Villas Ltd v Diamond Resorts Ltd (2018)** seems to have settled many of the arguments by holding that timeshare property owners enjoyed the benefit of easements to use sporting facilities and communal gardens surrounding their property. The court confirmed **Re Ellenborough Park** on this point.

5.18 Any claimed recreational easement must still satisfy the Ellenbrough Park criteria, particularly that the recreational easement must accommodate the dominant tenement. Each case will turn on its facts, but Regency Villas was an easier case to satisfy because it was a holiday timeshare property where leisure facilities might well benefit the timeshare properties.

(vii) May not be exclusive possession

5.19 An easement should not mean that the servient owner is denied the use of their land. However, some easements can amount to an exclusive use by the dominant owner, especially where the easement is one of storage (**Wright v Macadam (1949)**) or parking (**Batchelor v Marlow (2003)**).

5.20 The courts have considered whether the use by the dominant owner amounts to exclusive possession. In **Batchelor v Marlow (2003)**, the CA set down the **'degree' test** asking whether the right granted would leave the servient owner with any **reasonable use of their land**. If it does not, then it is not an easement. However, this test appears less favoured than that set down by a Scottish appeal to the House of Lords in **Moncrieff v Jamieson (2008)** where the **'possession and control' test** was used. Does the servient owner retain possession and control of their land where there is reasonable use of the easement by the dominant owner? If so, then there will be an easement.

5.21 Naturally, the court is seeking to strike a balance between allowing valid easements, without undermining the ownership of the servient owner. As to which test should be followed, technically, the test from Batchelor is binding, but the law on easements in England is substantially the same as its Scottish counterpart (servitudes), so Moncrieff could be easily applicable in England and Wales.

Positive and Negative Easements

5.22 As stated, easements can be positive and negative and they may develop as society and circumstances develop; the categories of easements are not closed (**Dyce v Lady Hay (1852)**). While the courts have been willing to recognise new, novel, positive easements, eg, to use land to move aircraft (**Dowty Boulton Paul Ltd v Wolverhampton Corporation (No 2) (1976)**), and to hang washing (**Drewell v Towler (1832)**), recognising new negative easements is something more of a challenge (**Phipps v Pears (1964)**).

Acquisition of Easements

5.23 Once a right claimed has the characteristics of an easement, the next stage is to determine whether the interest has been **acquired as an easement**. An easement might be acquired in a number of ways:

(i) Express grant or reservation;

(ii) Implied grant or reservation;

    (a) Common intention;

    (b) Necessity;

(iii) Rule in Wheeldon v Burrows (Grant only);

(iv) Section 62, Law of Property Act 1925 (Grant

only);

(v)   Prescription.

5.24 Before considering these in detail, it is first necessary to make clear the **terminology** of **grant** and **reservation**.

5.25 To **grant is to give a right**, while to **reserve is to keep a right**. For example, Andy owns Blackacre and Greenacre. They are adjoining properties. Andy leased Blackacre to Carey. In the lease, Andy gave (granted) Carey the right to cross over Greenacre so Carey could access a garage. Here, Andy **granted the easement** to Carey. Andy's land is the servient land, and Carey's land the dominant land.

5.26 Alternatively, if, in the same scenario, Andy needed access over Blackacre to get to the main road, Andy would retain (reserve) a right to cross Blackacre from Greenacre to get to the main road. Here, Andy **reserves an easement of way** to cross Blackacre. Andy's land is the dominant land, and Carey's land is the servient land.

(i)   Express grant or reservation

5.27 An expressly granted or reserved easement is one which has been deliberately created by an individual. It is expressed in the document which creates the transfer. In paragraph 5.24, above, there is an example of an express grant. In paragraph 5.25, above, there is an example of an express reservation.

(ii)   Implied grant or reservation

5.28 Where the parties haven't considered the easement, one may be **implied into the document creating the transfer**. Some easements may be implied by **grant or reservation**, namely **common intention** and **necessity**, whereas some operate in **grant only**, namely the **rule in Wheeldon v Burrows, section 62, LPA 1925**, and **prescription**.

(ii) *Implied grant or reservation – Common intention*

5.29 Implied easements by common intention give effect to the common intention of transferor and transferee. For an easement to be implied, the claimant needs to show that the easement was in the contemplation of the parties at the date of transfer and that the easement is necessary to give effect to that common intention. The parties must have intended the land to be used in a particular way (**Stafford v Lee (1992)**).

5.30 In **Stafford v Lee (1992)**, the claimant (Stafford) obtained planning permission to build a house on his land. The only access for construction traffic was across the defendant's (Lee's) land. The claimant sought a declaration from the court that such traffic had access across the defendant's land, but also that there would be future access for all purposes connected with the land. In granting the declaration, the court held that it was the common intention of the parties that Stafford's land should enjoy an easement over Lee's land. Nourse LJ found the requisite intention in the plan attached to the conveyance. It demonstrated that since similarly sized plots as that which was conveyed to Stafford already had dwellings on them, the balance of convenience indicated that can only have been the intention of the parties.

(ii) *Implied grant or reservation – Necessity*

5.31 Implied easements by necessity are used where, without the easement, the land would not be possible to use. The most common example is that of land which, without the easement, would otherwise be landlocked. However, this method of acquisition is narrowly construed, so even if a less convenient means of access to land is available, an easement of necessity will not be implied, as demonstrated by **Manjang v Drammeh (1990)**. In Manjang, the land which was bordered on three sides by land belonging to others, but was accessible on its fourth side by the River Gambia, a publicly navigable river, was denied an easement of necessity over neighbouring land.

(iii)   Rule in Wheeldon v Burrows (Grant only)

5.32 This method of acquisition operates in grant *only*. It is best illustrated by an example. Suppose Alan owns two neighbouring plots of land called Blackacre and Greenacre. In order to get to Greenacre, Alan uses a road which crosses Blackacre. If Blackacre and Greenacre were owned by different people, whoever owned Greenacre would enjoy an easement over Blackacre. However, they are not owned by different people, they are both owned by Alan, so it cannot be an easement. Let's suppose now that Alan is in need of money so he sells Greenacre to Callum, without giving Callum access across Blackacre so Callum can get to Greenacre. In such circumstances, so long as the requirements from **Wheeldon v Burrows (1879)** are met, the quasi-easement across Blackacre which Alan previously used to get to Greenacre, would pass to Callum as the new owner of Greenacre as a full easement. The requirements of **Wheeldon v Burrows** are that a quasi-easement will pass as a full easement to the new owner of the relevant land where the following criteria are met:

(a)   The use of the quasi-easement was continuous and apparent;

(b)   It was necessary for the reasonable enjoyment of the land granted; and,

(c)   It was used by the grantor for the benefit of the land granted.

5.33 Let's consider each of these elements in a little more detail.

(a)   The use of the quasi-easement was continuous and apparent

5.34 An easement is **continuous** if it is the right to do something which is **continuous in nature**. An **apparent** easement is one which is **obvious from examination of the**

land by a person ordinarily conversant with the subject. For example, drains and paths might be continuous and apparent (**Ward v Kirkland (1967)**), as well as a right to light through a defined window (**Phillips v Low (1892)**), a right of way defined by tarmacked roadway (**Hillman v Rogers (1998)**), and an underground drain into which water runs from the eaves of a house (**Watts v Kelson (1870)**; **McAdams Homes Ltd v Robinson (2004)**).

(b)   It was necessary for the reasonable enjoyment of the land granted

5.35 There is some debate in this area over the words **necessary** and **reasonable** and how they relate to **continuous and apparent**. It would seem, following recent cases, that **continuous and apparent** does not stand alone but should be read alongside this requirement (**Alford v Hannaford (2011)(CA)**; **Wood v Waddington (2015)(CA)**). In terms of *reasonably necessary*, it appears that the emphasis rests on the word **reasonable** (**Wheeler v JJ Saunders (1996)(CA)**).

(c)   It was used by the grantor for the benefit of the land granted

5.36 This is fairly self-explanatory in that the quasi-easement must be in use by the grantor at the date of the transfer. Interestingly, in **Kent v Kavanagh (2007)(CA)**, a claim to an easement was rejected because the quasi-easement was in use by a tenant at the time of the transfer.

(iv)   Section 62, Law of Property Act 1925 (Grant only)

5.37 Section 62, LPA 1925 is a word-saving provision used by conveyancers and ensures that conveyances include all those things one might expect to be included, particularly for our purposes, it includes rights, easements, etc. However, s62, LPA 1925 has been held to have the curious effect of elevating a mere permission to an easement (**Wright v Macadam**

(1949); Hair v Gillman (2000)).

5.38 The section operates on the following conditions:

> (i) There must be a conveyance of a legal lease or freehold by deed;
>
> (ii) There must be evidence of prior use; AND,
>
> (iii) No contrary intention expressed (**s62(4), LPA 1925**).

5.39 Previously, it was thought that prior diversity of occupation was needed (**Sovmots Investments Ltd v Secretary of State for the Environment (1979)**), but this no longer seems to be the case (**P & S Platt Ltd v Crouch (2004)(CA)**, confirmed in **Wood v Waddington (2015)(CA)**).

5.40 The decision in **P & S Platt Ltd v Crouch (2004)(CA)**, by doing away with the requirement of prior diversity of occupation, does bring into question the continuing significance of the rule in Wheeldon v Burrows, but the detail will need to be hammered out over the next few years in the case law. However, Wheeldon v Burrows was applied in the recent Tribunal decision of **Taurusbuild Ltd v McQue (2019)**, where it passed a quasi-easement to a mortgagee in possession, which was then subsequently passed to a purchaser of the repossessed property, the McQues, by s62, LPA 1925. So, this case demonstrates the two methods can work alongside one another.

(v)   Prescription

5.41 The final method of acquiring an easement is by **prescription**, or **long use**. This method has it that so long as it can be shown that an easement has been in use for some time, the easement might operate by this method.

5.42 There are three ways of establishing an easement by long use:

(i)   Common Law;

(ii) Doctrine of Lost Modern Grant;

(iii) Prescription Act 1832.

(i)   Common Law

5.43 At common law, it is presumed the grant of easement was made before 1189 (the date of legal memory), unless it can be shown not to have existed at the time, or could not have existed at some point since that time.

5.44 To bring the claim, it must be shown that the use was **without force**, **without secrecy**, and **without permission**, but proving common law prescription is difficult.

(ii)   Doctrine of Lost Modern Grant

5.45 The doctrine of lost modern grant supplements the common law position making a presumption that the grant was made in the past but has been lost, hence, *lost modern grant*. A period of 20 years use must be shown, but it does not have to have immediately preceded the claim.

(iii)   Prescription Act 1832

5.46 Under the Prescription Act 1832, there are two designated periods of time: 20 years and 40 years. If a right has been established for **40 years**, it is deemed **absolute and indefeasible**. If the right is by the 20 year period, it cannot be defeated merely by showing that it cannot have existed at some point since 1189.

5.47 The claim must be as of right, and must be for the period immediately preceding the claim, unlike with the doctrine of lost modern grant.

5.48 Where an **easement of light** is concerned, the right is deemed **absolute and indefeasible** where the right has been enjoyed for **20 years without interruption**, unless enjoyed by agreement or consent.

Formalities and Protection of Easements

5.49 As with everything in land law, the scheme of protection of interests must be considered. Naturally, the answer will differ depending on whether title to the land is **registered** or **unregistered**. Additionally, it is also important to consider the formalities in the creation of easements.

Express Legal Easements

5.50 An express legal easement is an interest in land under s1(2)(a), LPA 1925, provided they are granted for the equivalent of a freehold or leasehold estate. It would need to be by deed (s52, LPA 1925; s1, LP(MP)A 1989) and once created, in order to be **binding in registered title**, would need to be **substantively registered** (s27, Land Registration Act 2002). Where title is **unregistered**, as a legal interest, it **would bind the whole world**.

Implied Legal Easements

5.51 An implied legal easement is implied into the document creating the transfer, ie, a deed. In order for implied legal easements to be binding on a purchaser of the land where title is registered, **there is nothing to do**! Why? Well, implied legal easements override under sch3, para3, Land Registration Act 2002. In other words, they are binding without the need for registration. Where title is **unregistered**, as a legal interest, it **would bind the whole world**.

Express Equitable Easements

5.52 This is an equitable interest under s1(3), LPA 1925. Generally, such easements must comply with s2, LP(MP)A 1989, unless they were a consciously created equitable easement at the outset, in which case complying with s53(1)(a), LPA 1925 will suffice. Once created, in order to be **binding in registered title**, it would need to be protected as a **notice on charges register** (s32, LRA 2002) otherwise, a purchaser takes free of it (s29, LRA 2002). Where **title** is **unregistered**, it would be protected as either a **D(iii)** or **C(iv) Land Charge**, otherwise the purchaser takes free of it (s4(6), Land Charges Act 1972).

Implied Equitable Easements

5.53 Such easements are, once again, implied into the relevant document which created the easement. Once implied, in order to be **binding in registered title**, it would need to be protected as a **notice on charges register** (s32, LRA 2002) otherwise, a purchaser takes free of it (s29, LRA 2002). Where **title** is **unregistered**, it would be protected as either a **D(iii)** or **C(iv) Land Charge**, otherwise purchaser takes free of it (s4(6), Land Charges Act 1972).

Profits à prendre

5.54 A profit à prendre (or profit, for short) is the right to take something from another's land. A good example is the right to shoot or fish another's land. A profit may be granted by the landowner by deed, or it may be acquired by prescription at common law, or by the doctrine of lost modern grant. A profit may not, however, be found under prescription as set down in the Prescription Act 1832. A profit is capable of being registered with its own title under the Land Registration Act 2002.

CHAPTER 6
MORTGAGES

Introduction

6.01 A mortgage is an interest in land (s1(2)(c), LPA 1925). In plain language, it is a sum of money advanced in return for security over a house. The mortgagor (borrower), grants the security over their house to the mortgagee (lender).

The Equity of Redemption

6.02 At common law, the borrower had to repay the mortgage on the legal date of redemption, ie, the legal date for repayment set down in the contract. Failure to repay on this fixed date entitled the lender to the property. This was harsh, such that equity intervened to create the equity of redemption. This is the idea that so long as the borrower repaid the money as required, the lender could not claim the property; 'once a mortgage, always a mortgage' (Lord Parker in **Kreglinger v New Patagonia Meat and Cold Storage Company (1915)** AC 25). Over time, the equity of redemption has also been taken to mean the totality of the rights enjoyed by the borrower:

(i)   the right not to be subject to a postponed date of redemption;

(ii) the right to be free of options to purchase;

(iii) the right to be free of collateral advantages;

(iv) the right to be free from unconscionable terms.

(i)   postponed date of redemption

6.03 If the lender imposes a date of redemption so far into the future it makes the right to redeem illusory, it will not be binding on the borrower. In **Fairclough v Swan Brewery Co Ltd (1912)**, a clause in a lease postponing the date of redemption until six weeks before the lease expired was void, whereas in **Knightsbridge Estates Trust Ltd v Byrne (1939)**, postponement for 40 years from the date of the loan was upheld as the parties to the transaction were commercial parties.

6.04 The power to redeem a mortgage is contained in s91, LPA 1925.

(ii) option to purchase

6.05 When a mortgage is given, the lender cannot insist on an option to purchase the property (**Samuel v Jarrah Timber and Wood Paving Corporation Ltd (1904)**), unless it is granted after the mortgage so it can be regarded as an independent transaction (**Reeve v Lisle (1902)**). However, this is not a fixed rule, as the CA in **Warnborough Ltd v Garmite Ltd (2004)** indicated. In that case transactions on the same day were regarded as separate.

(iii) collateral advantages

6.06 When a mortgage is given, the lender cannot also claim other things in addition to the right to repayment, ie, collateral advantages. For example, in **Noakes & Co Ltd v Rice (1902)**, a tenant landlord of a pub was required to purchase certain alcohol only from the lender, even after the mortgage was repaid. The court held the clause to be void. Contrast **Biggs v Hoddinott (1898)**, where a similar arrangement was limited to the mortgage period and so was valid. Sometimes, agreements to continue *after* the mortgage term will be upheld, so long as it was a proper commercial transaction to the benefit of both parties (**Kreglinger v New Patagonia Meat & Cold Storage Co Ltd (1914)**).

(iv) unconscionable terms

6.07 Unconscionable terms is a broad phrase, and includes collateral advantages, but it also covers excessive rates of interest (**Cityland and Property Holdings Ltd v Dabrah (1968)**). However, where the parties enter into a transaction with their eyes wide open, understanding the terms of the mortgage, the courts will not intervene, no matter how oppressive the term (**Multiservice Bookbinding Ltd v Marden (1978)**).

6.08 Unconscionable terms relating to the rate of interest charged on a mortgage are governed by the unfair relationships test in s140A, Consumer Credit Act 1974 (as amended).

6.09 Additionally, the Law of Property Act 1925 gives the borrower further statutory rights:

> Section 91 – gives the borrower a power to redeem the mortgage which can be enforced by the court;
>
> Section 99 – gives the borrower a power to lease the property for certain purposes and the power to accept surrenders of existing leases. This power may be modified by the terms of the mortgage;
>
> Section 98 – gives the borrower power to claim possession of the mortgaged property where the mortgagee does not claim possession;
>
> Sections 91(1) and 91(2) – These provisions allow a borrower to apply to the court for an order for sale of the property which the court may decide to grant even if the mortgagee is opposed (**Palk v Mortgage Services Funding plc (1993)**). This right to apply is important where the borrower cannot pay instalments due on a mortgage causing the debt to mount up. A sale at this time can be advantageous, even if the house sells for less than the outstanding mortgage (negative equity), as it can prevent debts mounting up; this is what happened in *Palk*.

Enforcing a mortgage – the rights and remedies of the mortgagee

6.10 The lender enjoys a number of rights and remedies under a mortgage:

(i) right to possession;

(ii) power of sale;

(iii) appointment of a receiver;

(iv) foreclosure;

(i) possession

6.11 A lender has the right to take possession of the mortgaged property (s95(4), LPA 1925), or *before the ink is dry on the mortgage* (**Four Maids Ltd v Dudley Marshall (Properties) Ltd (1957)**). Possession might be effected either by **court order** or by taking **peaceful possession**.

Court order

6.12 Where possession is taken by court order, the borrower may attempt to resist the application by recourse to s36, Administration of Justice Act 1970. The provision gives the court a *power* to adjourn the proceedings, or stay or suspend execution of the judgment or postpone the date for possession if the house is: (1) a dwelling or *includes* a dwelling and (2) it appears the borrower is likely to be able to pay any sums due under the mortgage within a reasonable period. A "reasonable period" is the remainder of the mortgage term (**Cheltenham and Gloucester Building Society v Norgan (1996)**). The borrower must present a viable financial plan to the court (**National and Provincial Building Society v Lloyd (1996)**).

6.13 A postponement may permit the borrower to sell the property (**Target Home Loans Ltd v Clothier (1994)**), but only where there is clear evidence to support it (**Mortgage Service Funding plc v Steele (1996)**). In the current housing market, ie, where prices are falling or stagnant, postponement may not be granted if it were to prejudice a lender (**Cheltenham and Gloucester plc v Krausz (1997)**).

Peaceful possession

6.14 It is possible for the lender to take possession by peaceful possession (**Ropaigealach v Barclays Bank plc (1999)**). One advantage to the lender of peaceful possession is that s36, AJA 1970 does not apply. However, the lender should take care not to commit an offence under s6, Criminal Law Act 1977 (threaten violence for the purpose of securing entry).

(ii) power of sale

6.15 The power of sale is contained in every mortgage (s101, LPA 1925) which arises when the mortgage money is due. However, it only becomes exercisable under s103, LPA 1925 where (a) notice requiring repayment of capital has been served by the lender *and* the borrower has defaulted for three months after service; or (b) any interest under the mortgage is in arrears and unpaid for at least two months; or (c) there has been a breach of some other mortgage provision, either express or implied by the LPA 1925.

Mortgagee's duties on sale

6.16 When selling the property, the lender is under a duty to take reasonable care to obtain a proper price, dependent on the circumstances of the case (**Newport Farm Ltd v Damesh Holdings Ltd (2003)**). Reasonable care includes selling within the appropriate price bracket (**Michael v Miller (2004)**), and advertising any obtained planning permissions when selling the property (**Cuckmere Brick Co Ltd v Mutual Finance Ltd (1971)**). However, the lender is under no obligation to improve the property prior to sale (**Silven Properties Ltd v Royal Bank of Scotland plc (2003)**).

6.17 Another important issue is **when to sell?** At the moment, the market is stale or stagnant so it might be advisable to wait until the market picks up. In **Standard Chartered Bank Ltd v Walker (1982)**, the CA said *obiter* that the lender had to exercise reasonable care in deciding when to sell, although **Cuckmere Brick Co Ltd v Mutual Finance Ltd (1971)** and **China and South Sea Bank Ltd v Tan Soon Gin (1990)** suggest the contrary; the lender can sell the property when he likes. An interesting case in this area is **Palk v Mortgage Services Funding plc (1993)**, where the lender wanted to ride out the market and wait for an improvement. However, the court permitted the borrower to force sale on the basis that the arrears would have accrued at £30,000 per year.

6.18 Where the sale realises more than the mortgage debt, any surplus is held on trust for the borrower (s105, LPA 1925)).

(iii) appointment of receiver

6.19 A lender might appoint a receiver under a power in s101, LPA 1925. When appointed, the receiver becomes the borrower's agent, meaning the lender is not liable for the receiver's acts. In **Medforth v Blake (2000)**, a receiver running a pig farm was liable for failing to negotiate a discount for the purchase of pig food.

(iv) foreclosure

6.20 This is the remedy of last resort since it seizes all of the borrower's rights and gives them to the lender. It is a remedy little used today.

Undue Influence

6.21 If one party to the mortgage agreement has been coerced or pressured into signing the mortgage agreement, they may be able to avoid enforcement of the mortgage by showing that they were subject to undue influence by another before signing the contract.

6.22 Much of the modern law on undue influence has been

concerned with cases where joint owners of property enter into a joint mortgage where one party was pressured into agreeing it by the other co-owner.

6.23 In **Royal Bank of Scotland v Etridge (No 2) (2001)**, HL sought to clarify the law. There are two broad categories of undue influence: **Actual undue influence** and **presumed undue influence**.

Actual undue influence

6.24 In contrast to situations of presumed undue influence, actual undue influence must be proved against a party because it is not a 'traditional' relationship where undue influence might be presumed (**BCCI v Aboody (1990)**). Naturally, where the situation is one of presumed undue influence, the claimant would be best advised to use that option, especially given the evidential difficulties of proving actual undue influence.

Presumed undue influence

6.25 Certain relationships might call transactions into question and give rise to a presumption meaning the contract requires explanation. These include, but are not limited to, doctor-patient, parent-child, trustee-beneficiary. The presumption might be rebutted where evidence is presented that the party took independent legal advice.

6.26 The relationship between husband and wife is not one where the presumption arises. Evidence is needed to demonstrate that one party exerts pressure over another.

6.27 As indicated, much of the modern law in this area has arisen in the context of joint mortgages between married couples. Usually, but not always, the husband will pressure the wife into signing the mortgage agreement. If the bank has notice of undue influence, it will only be able to enforce the mortgage in the event of default if it took reasonable steps to advise the wife as to the consequences of default and, also, that she should take independent legal advice of the transaction.

The importance of lenders complying with the guidelines from Etridge was emphasised in the recent case of **HSBC Bank plc v Brown (2015)**.

6.28 Thus, the obligation might then shift to the legal adviser who should explain the documentation, the risks involved, and advise the person they have a choice.

Mortgages *postscript*

6.29 As the creation and protection of estates and interests in land moves into the 21st century, and more legal documentation is created and processed electronically, the Land Registry announced in October 2019 that a total of 1,000 mortgage deeds have now been signed and registered digitally. This is a sign of the future of conveyancing, but it has been a long time in the making. Expect more developments in this context over the next decade, especially as the use of blockchain technology is developed in this area.

CHAPTER 7
PROPRIETARY ESTOPPEL

Introduction

7.01 Much of English land law is concerned with the formal acquisition of estates and interests, but there are some ways of **acquiring property rights informally**, and **proprietary estoppel** is one of them.

7.02 In essence, a proprietary estoppel arises where one party makes an **assurance** about a property right, and the party to whom it is made acts in **reliance** on that assurance to their **detriment**. Once these elements are satisfied, the court has discretion to award a remedy.

7.03 Thus, the elements of proprietary estoppel are:

(i) An individual makes an **assurance (or representation)**, a **promise**, or **encourages** another to believe, or **acquiesces** in a misunderstanding, that another will enjoy some right;

(ii) The recipient will then place **reliance** on that assurance, etc;

(iii) Which reliance is **detrimental** to the recipient;

(iv) The maker of the assurance, etc, then acts unconscionably in seeking to deny the right promised.

Gillett v Holt (2000)(CA); Thorner v Major (2009)(HL)

7.04 Although these elements are cited separately, remember we are dealing with an equitable concept here, so flexibility is key, even in application of the principles (**Taylor Fashions v**

Liverpool Victoria Trustees Co (1981)).

(i)   An individual makes an assurance, etc

7.05 An individual must make some form of assurance (representation) that the person has or will have some right or interest, in this context, in relation to land. The assurance can be one about the freehold estate (**Gillett v Holt (2000)**), or an interest in land, eg, an easement over land (**Crabb v Arun DC (1976)**). General or vague assurances, such as suggesting that the recipient will always have a roof over their head will not be sufficient (**Coombes v Smith (1986)**), though assurances as to the future receipt of property, such as by will, can be sufficient. So, in **Re Basham (1986)**, an assurance that a step-daughter would inherit a freehold estate from her step-father was a sufficient assurance.

7.06 The examples in the cases discussed so far are good examples of **active assurances**, where one party encourages another to form a belief. However, acquiescence (**passive assurance**) may be enough where the recipient is mistaken or misunderstands, which the other party realises, but does then not correct the recipient (**Ramsden v Dyson (1866)**).

7.07 Fundamentally, the assurance or promise must be sufficiently clear (**Thorner v Major (2009)(HL)**), when looked at objectively (**Gillett v Holt (2002)(CA)**), and may change over the course of the period relevant to the estoppel claim. So, in the recent case of **Guest v Guest (2019)**, the High Court upheld a proprietary estoppel claim, even where what the claimant expected to obtain changed from sole ownership of the farm to joint ownership when the claimant's brother started to work on the farm under similar assurances.

(ii)   The recipient will then place reliance on that assurance, etc

7.08 Once the assurance has been made, the recipient must act in reliance on that assurance, and the **reliance must be reasonable**, and will be judged objectively. In essence, the requirement is the **causal link** between the assurance and what follows (**Gillett v Holt (2000)**).

7.09 Whether the reliance is reasonable will be a question which relies heavily on the facts but ongoing contractual negotiations (**Haq v Island Homes Housing Association and another (2011)**) and sensitive business relations conducted between professionals are unlikely to give rise to a proprietary estoppel as reliance may not be reasonable (**Yeoman's Row Management Ltd v Cobbe (2008)**).

(iii)   Which reliance is detrimental to the recipient

7.10 Importantly, the reliance, as well as being reasonable, has to be **detrimental** to the recipient or, exceptionally, the detriment of another, eg, a husband on which a wife then based a claim (**Matharu v Matharu (1994)**).

7.11 The detriment must be significant, but it can be monetary or, more usually in estoppel cases, some other form of quantifiable non-monetary detriment (**Gillett v Holt (2000)**). Detriment can overlap with the causal element of the reliance requirement giving greater strength to the argument that the assurance caused the recipient to rely to their detriment (**Gillett v Holt (2000)(CA)**; **Cook v Thomas (2010)(CA)**).

7.12 There are many examples from case law for what has been accepted as detrimental to the recipient. For example, where the recipient pays for improvements to the other's property (**Pascoe v Turner (1979)**), or constructs new buildings on the other's land (**Inwards v Baker (1965)**). Alternatively, one party has cared for an individual for no or little payment (**Grundy v Ottey (2003)**), or worked for another for little or no payment for a number of years (**Greasley v Cooke (1980)**; **Gillett v Holt (2000)**).

(iv)   The maker of the assurance, etc, then acts unconscionably in seeking to deny the right promised

7.13 Where the elements are made out and the individual who made the assurance then tries to deny the rights to the recipient, this will be regarded as unconscionable and equity will intervene to prevent the wrong from being committed.

Remedy

7.14 The elements, once made out, **give rise to an equity**, which is **satisfied by the award of a remedy**. Importantly, the **remedy is flexible**, allowing the court considerable **discretion** either to award the thing promised, or compensation, or something else. Generally, it is deemed to be the **minimum necessary to do justice (Jennings v Rice (1992))**.

7.15 Naturally, because of flexibility and the discretion, it is difficult to be definitive on what the court will award, so looking at the cases can provide useful guidance.

7.16 In **Pascoe v Turner (1979)**, the recipient was promised the house, so legal title was transferred to them as the remedy. In **Greasley v Cooke (1980)**, the assurance was that the recipient could remain in a house for the rest of her life, and the court gave her the right to live there for the rest of her life. In **Crabb v Arun DC (1976)**, Crabb was promised a right of access over land he sold to the council, which the council denied after Crabb sold the land. The court upheld the assurance and gave Crabb the right of access. A similar outcome occurred in the case of (**Hoyl Group v Cromer Town Council (2015)**).

7.17 In some circumstances, the recipient will not always get what they expected on the basis of the 'assurance'. In **Jennings v Rice (2002)(CA)**, the court said account should be taken between **expectation** and the **reliance** and that the remedy should be **proportionate** to reflect any difference between the two. Therefore, they awarded £200,000 even though the recipient had been promised a house valued at £435,000. The figure awarded represented the value of the work done.

7.18 The approach of giving a figure representing the work done was taken in **Habberfield v Habberfield (2018)**, where a daughter had worked for little or no wages on her father's farm on the assurance she would, one day, receive the farm. The farm was worth more than the value of the recipient's reliance (approximately 10 times more), so she was awarded a sum of money in compensation; the remedy was proportionate. This part of the decision was upheld by the CA in 2019.

Status of a proprietary estoppel

7.19 A proprietary estoppel is capable of binding third parties who purchase land which is subject to the proprietary estoppel. Where title is registered, s116 Land Registration Act 2002 makes the point that such interests are capable of binding third parties. It should be registered as a notice on the charges register of the burdened land (s32, LRA 2002), unless it is an interest which overrides by actual occupation under schedule 3, LRA 2002. Where title is unregistered it should be protected in the correct way (s6, Land Charges Act 1972), until the court order is effected (**Ives (ER) Investment Ltd v High (1967)**).

CHAPTER 8
TRUSTS OF LAND

Introduction

8.01 This is an area of law which has a significant amount of statute in it, but before we get to that, you need to understand the trust concept. A **trust** is an **equitable obligation** where **legal title is given to a trustee** and **equitable title is held by the beneficiary**. Equitable title is also known as the beneficial title.

8.02 Expressed as a diagram, it might look something like this one:

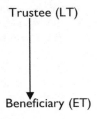

Trustee (LT)

Beneficiary (ET)

8.03 In the diagram, there is one trustee (holding legal title ('LT')) and one beneficiary (holding equitable title ('ET')), but there can be multiple trustees (but no more than four: s34(2), Trustee Act 1925), and multiple beneficiaries. Thus, a common situation in land law, where a couple buy a house together, they are both trustees and both beneficiaries.

8.04 The following cannot be emphasised enough: When a trust of land is created, there is a **separation of ownership between a legal owner and an equitable owner**. It is also important to understand **that the equitable title is a property right** and it gives the holder the right, *generally speaking*, to do with the equitable interest as they like. For example, the beneficiary could sell the equitable interest, or give it away.

Single Legal Owner

8.05 A single (outright) owner of land may create (declare) a trust and create an equitable interest for another. Thus there would be **one legal owner and a different equitable (or beneficial) owner**, or the **legal owner could create (declare) a trust and create an equitable interest for himself and another jointly**. If he created either trusts mentioned, he would need to comply with a statutory formality under **s53(1)(b), LPA 1925**, because either would be an **express declaration of a trust of land**. The statutory formality requires that an **express declaration of a trust of land must be evidenced by signed writing**. If this is not complied with, the **declaration will be unenforceable** because the claimant will not have the evidence to prove it.

Joint Legal Owners

8.06 Where land is purchased jointly, eg, by two people, the purchase takes effect as a trust of land, where both are legal owners, and both are equitable owners.

Trusts of Land and Appointment of Trustees Act 1996 ('ToLATA 1996')

8.07 Trusts which contain land as any part of the trust property, are **trusts of land** and governed by the provisions of ToLATA. It came into force on 1st January 1997, but applies to all trusts whenever they were created (ss2(1), 2(3), ToLATA).

8.08 The Act confers **powers on the trustees in relation to land, rights on the beneficiaries**, and wide **powers on the courts**. These are now considered.

Trustees' Powers in relation to land

8.09 The trustees are given all the powers of an absolute owner. In other words, they have the powers of a person who owns the land outright. This means that they can buy a property for the beneficiary to live in (s6, ToLATA). However, the powers under s6, ToLATA may be amended or excluded by the document which creates the trust.

Beneficiaries' Rights in relation to land

8.10 A beneficiary of full age, sound mind, and with an interested under the trust which is in possession must be consulted by the trustees. The consultation is in relation to the exercise of powers, etc, and the trustees must give effect to the wishes of the beneficiaries where they comply with the trust as a whole (s11, ToLATA).

8.11 Where there is a dispute between the beneficiaries, it should be resolved by majority determined by ownership rights.

8.12 Naturally, the beneficiary under a trust is entitled to occupy the land (s12, ToLATA), though this may be restricted by reference to the trust terms.

Courts' Powers under ToLATA

8.13 The court has extremely wide powers under ToLATA (**Bagum v Hafiz (2015)**), provided the powers are engaged by an application from a *person with an interest under a trust of land* (14, ToLATA). This could be a trustee, a beneficiary, a mortgagee (if a mortgage had been granted over the land), or the trustee in bankruptcy of a bankrupt beneficiary.

8.14 The nature of the order which the court makes is only really limited by the imagination of the judge, since the court may make such order as **it thinks fit in relation to the trustees' exercise of their functions**, and **the nature and extent of a person's interest in the trust property**.

8.15 When considering a s14 application, the court must have regard to the s15 criteria in making its determination. The criteria under s15(3), ToLATA are:

(a) the intentions of the person(s) who created the trust;

(b) the purposes for which the trust property is to be held. For example, sale will not be ordered where the original purpose endures (**Re Buchanan-Wollaston's Conveyance (1939)**).

(c) the welfare of any minor who occupies or might reasonably be expected to occupy any land as his home;

(d) the interests of any secured creditor of any beneficiary.

8.16 Under s15(3), ToLATA, the circumstances and wishes of any beneficiaries of full age and, where in dispute, those of the 'majority' are considered.

8.17 The most common form of order applied for under s14 is an **order for sale**, but they could make an order compelling the physical division of land between the co-owners (**Ellison v Cleghorn (2013)**).

Occupation rent

8.18 Under ToLATA, the court may award occupation rent (which used to be known as equitable accounting), to a beneficiary who has been excluded from the house which they have a right to occupy. This happened in the cases of **Stack v Dowden (2007)** and **Jones v Kernott (2011)**.

CHAPTER 9
TRUSTS OF THE HOME

Introduction

9.01 Trusts of the home has undergone radical judicial reform since the decision of the House of Lords in **Stack v Dowden (2007)**. This decision, together with the Supreme Court decision of **Jones v Kernott (2011)**, and the cases which have subsequently applied both, mean the question of home ownership can now be approached more flexibly than in the past.

Background

9.02 If married or in a civil partnership, statute confers broad discretionary powers on judges to resolve questions of ownership of property, namely the Matrimonial Causes Act 1973 and the Civil Partnerships Act 2004, respectively. But what happens when couples are not in a formal relationship and later separate? What happens when such couples buy a house together? Or, one moves into the other's house?

9.03 This is an important social question because an increasing number of couples are declining to formalise their relationship. So, how does English law provide a solution? Well, the trust has been manipulated over the years in order to find a solution to the problem.

9.04 The starting point is to distinguish between cases where both parties are registered as the legal owners, so-called **joint names cases**, from those where only one of the parties is registered as the owner, namely, **single name cases**.

Express Declaration: Joint Names

9.05 Where the land has **joint legal owners**, then on transfer the TR1 land transfer form, part 10, provides the parties with an opportunity to declare their equitable ownership. They can be (a) **joint tenants**, (b) **tenants in common in equal shares**, or, (c) **hold it another way as they may stipulate**, where the parties can indicate their individual shares. Where this is done, it will be binding, even where one party has provided all the purchase money, but the property is conveyed to them as 'joint tenants' (**R v Hayes (2018)(CA)**).

9.06 It is not compulsory to complete this part of the TR1, and this generates problems. Baroness Hale in **Stack v Dowden (2007)(HL)** considered it should be compulsory. Indeed, she is not the first judge to bemoan the failure to complete part 10. If you want to see a judge 'shout' in a judgment, with the statement in upper case letters, take some time to read the immensely entertaining paragraph 44 of Ward LJ's judgment in **Carlton v Goodman (2002)(CA)**.

Express Declaration: Single Name

9.07 Where there is a **single legal owner**, ie, only one name is registered, a declaration of an express trust in favour of the non-legal owner would need to comply with **section 53(1)(b), Law of Property Act 1925**. This requires that the declaration be **evidenced by signed writing**. If this occurs, then the non-legal owner will have an enforceable beneficial interest. This could be done at the date of the conveyance or at a later date.

9.08 An express declaration is *generally* conclusive (**Pettitt v Pettitt (1969)**; **Goodman v Gallant (1986)**). In the case of **Pankhania v Chandegra (2012)**, the court declined to set aside an express trust unless there was **fraud, mistake**, or **undue influence**, though the earlier case of **Clarke v Meadus (2010)** permitted an express trust to be overridden by **proprietary estoppel**.

9.09 If there is no express declaration of trust, the **implied trust (Hodgson v Marks (1971))** or **proprietary estoppel** offer alternative solutions.

Implied Trusts

9.10 Two forms of implied trust are relevant for the rest of our discussion: the **resulting trust** and the **constructive trust**. It is worthwhile taking some time to think about such trusts

Resulting Trust

9.11 The **presumed resulting trust** used to play a significant role in allowing a party to establish an equitable interest in the home. This would arise where one party **provided the purchase money at the point of acquisition** but, for whatever reason, the legal title to the property would go into another's name. The party providing the purchase money would receive a beneficial interest in the land (**Bull v Bull (1955)**).

9.12 However, the presumption of a resulting trust came in for criticism in the family home context because of its focus on financial contributions, ignoring all other contributions. Given this, the House of Lords in **Stack v Dowden (2007)** and the Supreme Court in **Jones v Kernott (2011)** stated that the presumption of a resulting trust is **not appropriate in the domestic family home context**, though it may have some value in other scenarios, eg, a house purchase made by members of the same family for purposes of a buy-to-let investment (**Laskar v Laskar (2008)(CA)**), or where an agreement is made on the understanding that though the property goes into one party's name, the other party is intended to be beneficially entitled (**Tahir v Faizi (2019)**).

Constructive Trust

9.13 The constructive trust, though not traditionally used as a means of informally allocating ownership of the family home, began to be turned to this use in the middle of the 20th century. It has since been stretched as a concept, but is now the principal mechanism used in this area of law.

Joint Names

9.14 If joint legal owners of land fail to declare how the beneficial interests are held, by filling out part 10 of the TR1 (see 9.05, above), the starting point is **joint beneficial ownership** between the parties (**Stack v Dowden (2007); Jones v Kernott (2011)**), **both parties have an equal (50:50) equitable interest because they have a legal interest. Joint beneficial ownership is a presumption** which can be rebutted. Rebutting the presumption is difficult (per Lord Walker in **Stack v Dowden (2007)**), but it may be done at two stages:

 a) At the **point of acquisition** to show their common intention that a different beneficial ownership was intended; OR

 b) That the parties **later** changed their common intention in relation to beneficial ownership.

9.15 There are two questions to determine in joint names cases: First, do the parties have a common intention to vary the starting point of 50:50? If so, secondly, then what is the amount each party is to receive? This two-stage approach was approved in **Barnes v Phillips (2015)(CA)**.

Common intention to vary 50:50?

9.16 To determine if the common intention of the parties has changed, either at the point of acquisition *or* subsequently, the task is to look for the **actual intention** of the parties to vary 50:50, or to infer from their conduct a common intention to vary 50:50, either initially or subsequently.

9.17 In **Jones v Kernott (2011)**, the parties cashed in life insurance policies so Mr Kernott could afford to move out of the family home and purchase his own house. From that point, Ms Jones made all the payments in respect of the joint home, ie, the mortgage, the utility bills, and so on. Thus, the common intention varied at that later date.

9.18 Also, in **Barnes v Phillips (2015)(CA)**, a subsequent remortgage was entirely to the benefit of Mr Barnes and that after 2008, Ms Phillips made all the mortgage payments. Thus, it could be inferred from their conduct that there was a common intention to vary 50:50 ownership.

9.19 The factors relevant to determining changes in the common intention of the parties are set down in paragraph 69 of Baroness Hale's speech in **Stack v Dowden (2007)**:

- Advice received by the parties, or discussions which they had at the point of purchase;

- The purpose for which the property was purchased;

- Their motivation for purchasing the property jointly;

- The nature of the relationship between the parties;

- Whether there are children of the relationship for which the parties have a responsibility to provide a home;

- The way in which the parties arranged their finances, eg, did they have separate bank accounts?;

- The way in which the couple paid bills and other outgoings in relation to the property;

- Why one party was authorised to give a valid receipt for capital monies.

9.20 All these factors are equal, where one is not superior to another. However, in some cases, like **Stack v Dowden (2007)**, the courts have given significant weight to financial contributions in departing from 50:50, though the facts of that case are unique. In contrast, in **Fowler v Barron (2008)**, one party contributed nothing towards the purchase of the property either in terms of a deposit or mortgage payments, yet the court did **not** allow the presumption of joint beneficial ownership to be rebutted.

What amount is each party to receive?

9.21 One should start the inquiry as to how much by considering if it can be worked out from the actual or inferred (drawing on the factors in para 69 of Stack v Dowden (2007)) common intention of the parties. If not, then it is possible to **impute their fair share having regard to their whole course of dealing in relation to the property**. An **imputed intention** is one the parties never actually had, but is one which the court believes is fair (**Jones v Kernott (2011)**, approving **Oxley v Hiscocks (2004)(CA)**). This approach was confirmed by the Court of Appeal in **Barnes v Phillips (2015)**.

9.22 Imputing a share based on what is fair has been criticised as arbitrary and tending to produce inconsistencies (**Aspden v Elvy (2012)**), but it now seems reasonably well-established.

Single Name

9.23 Where one name is on the legal title, the presumption is that the legal owner owns the entire beneficial interest: **one legal owner, one beneficial owner**. A party claiming an interest (that is, the non-legal owner) will need to do two things:

a) Show that they have an interest in the land ('**acquisition issue**'); AND,

b) The size of that interest ('**quantification issue**').

9.24 This can be done by showing an express declaration of trust to comply with s53(1)(b), LPA 1925 (see, paras 9.07 –

9.08, above), or demonstrating that an implied trust exists, because s53(2), LPA 1925 suspends the formalities of s53(1)(b), LPA 1925 for such trusts. The two forms of implied trust are the resulting trust and the constructive trust, mentioned above at 9.10 – 9.13.

9.25 As indicated, the resulting trust has limited role in the domestic family home context (**Stack v Dowden (2007)**; **Jones v Kernott (2011)**), though it seems to remain for other situations (**Laskar v Laskar (2008)**). Consequently, we are really only concerned with the **constructive trust**.

9.26 For our purposes, there are two types of constructive trust: **express common intention constructive trust** ('**ECICT**'); and, **inferred common intention constructive trust ('ICICT')** (**Lloyd's Bank v Rosset (1991)**).

'acquisition issue': ECICT

9.27 The ECICT requires two things:

(i)   Express agreement, arrangement, or understanding in relation to ownership of the land; AND

(ii)   Detrimental reliance by the non-legal owner on the agreement, etc.

9.28 The express agreement as to ownership should be at the time of the purchase or *exceptionally* at some later date (**Lloyds Bank v Rosset (1991)**) and communicated between the parties (**Springette v Defoe (1992)**). The agreement has to relate to ownership of the land, not merely sharing it as a home. Therefore, in **Clough v Killey (1996)**, a statement that everything was shared '50:50' was sufficient, as was a commitment that everything was 'half yours' in **Hammond v Mitchell (1992)**.

9.29 Somewhat unusually, the courts have also allowed

'excuses' made by the legal owner to constitute an agreement. In such cases, the legal owner will make an excuse for **not** putting the non-legal owner on the legal title. For example, stating that the non-legal owner is 'too young' as in **Eves v Eves (1974)**, that any inclusion might prejudice a divorce settlement, as in **Grant v Edwards (1986)**, or that there are tax implications from being on legal title as in **Hammond v Mitchell (1992)**. In **Curran v Collins (2015)**, where the excuse related to the expense of two names being on the legal title, the court indicated that interpretation of the excuse is fact-sensitive, but should generally be coupled with a positive assertion the property would be jointly owned.

9.30 The express agreement should be followed by detrimental reliance (**Lloyds Bank v Rosset (1991)**; **Eves v Eves (1974)**). This is conduct which cannot otherwise be explained: why did they do it if they didn't think they were getting an interest in the property? (**Grant v Edwards (1986)**).

9.31 Detriment includes improvements to the family home (**Eves v Eves (1970)**), or indirect financial contributions to the household, without which, the legal owner could not pay the mortgage (**Grant v Edwards (1986)**; and in the ICICT context, **Le Foe v Le Foe (2001)**). Minor amendments and decoration (**Pettitt v Pettitt (1970)**) do not count as detrimental reliance.

'quantification issue': ECICT

9.32 Where there is an express agreement which makes clear the share each party is to have, *generally* that will be given effect. So, in **Clough v Killey (1992)** and **Hammond v Mitchell (1992)**, the parties were given half each. In **Williamson v Sheikh (2008)**, the court used an unsigned trust deed to determine the agreed share. However, where there has been express agreement as to ownership, but no statement as to the shares, it may be possible to infer an agreement. In **Gallarotti v Sebastianelli (2012)**, two friends bought a property together with an express agreement as to

50:50. This was later varied by inference that they were to share the property other than equally where S was awarded a greater share (75%) to account for the fact that S paid the mortgage contributions alone.

9.33 However, if there is no expressly agreed share, and it is not possible to infer from their conduct, then it may be possible for the court to impute shares where it is considered **fair having regard to the whole course of dealing between them in relation to the property**.

'acquisition issue': ICICT

9.34 Where there is no express common intention, it is possible to drawn an inference to share ownership from the parties' conduct in relation to the property. In **Lloyds Bank v Rosset (1991)**, Lord Bridge indicated that *only* contributions to mortgage payments would be sufficient to give rise to the inference. However, Baroness Hale in **Stack v Dowden (2007)** stated that set the threshold too high and that the **law had moved on** from that position.

9.35 It is possible that indirect financial contributions are sufficient if they are referable to the acquisition of the property (**Gissing v Gissing (1968)**). Also, where the contributions are to payment of bills, without which, the legal owner would not be able to afford the mortgage, then this may suffice (**Le Foe v Le Foe (2001)**). This is sometimes referred to as the 'family economy thesis'.

9.36 Further, substantial improvement to the property by DIY might be enough to infer an agreement to share ownership (obiter in **Stack v Dowden (2007)**). Also, in **Aspden v Elvy (2012)**, an inference was found where the direct financial contributions were made to the conversion of the property, rather than to its acquisition.

9.37 Perhaps the most significant development is the suggestion in the Privy Council case of **Abbott v Abbott (2007)** that the full range of paragraph 69 factors from **Stack v Dowden (2007)** (see, para 9.19, above), might be used when seeking to draw an inference as to sharing ownership of the home.

9.38 Before turning to the issue of quantification, it is worth noting that it is not possible to impute at this stage in the process, ie, 'acquisition' (**Capethorn v Harris (2015)(CA)**).

'quantification issue': ICICT

9.39 Generally, the inference will generate the amount to be shared. So, if the inference is equality, that will be the position. However, if nothing can be inferred, then, and only then, may the court impute by **having regard to the whole course of dealing between the parties in relation to the property** (**Oxley v Hiscocks (2004)**, approved in **Jones v Kernott (2011)**). This approach was taken in **Thompson v Hurst (2012)**, **Aspden v Elvy (2012)**, and **Graham-York v York (2015)**.

Proprietary Estoppel

9.40 A further means of establishing an interest in the home and which was certainly in prominent use prior to the changes made to the law by **Stack v Dowden (2007)** and **Jones v Kernott (2011)**, is proprietary estoppel. Prior to the changes brought about by Stack and Jones, proprietary estoppel offered a basis for reforming the law in this area (**Law Commission, Sharing Homes: Discussion Paper, Law Com No 278 (2002)**). While there is more detail in chapter seven on proprietary estoppel, here is a brief overview.

9.41 In **Thorner v Major (2009)(HL)**, it was stated that in order to establish proprietary estoppel, the claimant needed to show:

a) a representation made or assurance given to the claimant;

b) reliance by the claimant on the representation or

assurance; and,

c)   some detriment incurred by the claimant as a consequence of that reliance.

9.42 The assurance could be a clear representation, or passive encouragement. Clearly, the detriment would be fact-sensitive and not something which is limited to financial expenditure in reliance on the assurance.

9.43 In respect of remedy, the claimant will not necessarily receive what was promised in the assurance, though this is possible. The remedy will depend on the claimant's expectation and the detriment suffered, including the context. For example, in **Pascoe v Turner (1979)**, though the claimant's detriment was small, in the context of the claimant's overall (limited) wealth, it was in fact a significant detriment.

Reform

9.44 It is certainly the case that the law has been significantly reformed by judicial action since the decision of the House of Lords in **Stack v Dowden (2007)**, but is this the end of the matter? Possibly not. There has been an increase in cases before the courts since **Stack** as its limits are explored in order to produce settled principles. However, an approach which has 'fairness' in it will always result in some degree of uncertainty in case law, though it is doubtful a comprehensive statutory regime would produce a system which is any better as it would still need to be discretionary. This is the problem with an area of law such as this one. Legal rules and principles which are too strict may result in some semblance of injustice, as in **Burns v Burns (1984)**, whereas a system which places reasonable discretion in the hands of the judiciary may be difficult to apply consistently from case to case.

CHAPTER 10
COMMON OWNERSHIP

Introduction

10.01   Co-ownership (Common Ownership) arises where property is owned by at least two people. Most types of property might be co-owned, eg, a bank account (**Paul v Constance (1977)**), or a car, but in English law, co-ownership is examined in detail in relation to joint ownership of land. Therefore, co-ownership in land law occurs where two or more people own title to land.

Types of Co-ownership

10.02   In relation to land, co-ownership may operate either where land is owned **successively** or **concurrently**. Land might be owned under **successive interests** where, for example, land is given to A for life, with remainder to B. A will be able to live in the house for life, while B (or B's estate) will be able to enjoy the property when A dies. Land might be owned under **concurrent interests** where, for example, land is given to A and B. Each has the right to occupy the land at the same time. It is concurrent ownership of land that is our concern.

Basics of Co-ownership

10.03   Since 1st January 1997, the date on which the Trust of Land and Appointment of Trustees Act (ToLATA) 1996 came into force, all co-owned land takes effect as a trust of land. Where a trust is imposed, there is a **separation of legal and equitable title**. **Legal title** is owned by the **trustee**, while **equitable title** is owned by the **beneficiary**.

10.04   Co-owned land might be held as a joint tenancy or a tenancy in common. While **legal title might only be held**

as a joint tenancy (s1(6), Law of Property Act ('LPA') 1925) and by a **maximum** of **four legal owners** (s34(2), Trustee Act 1925; s34(2), LPA 1925) **equitable title** might be held as a **joint tenancy** or **tenancy in common**, and is capable of having many owners, though probably not so many that it would be administratively unworkable to manage the trust (**McPhail v Doulton (1970)(HL)**).

10.05 A **joint tenancy** exists where multiple owners are treated **as if they are one person** owning the land. Crucial to the joint tenancy is the existence of the four unities (**AG Securities v Vaughan (1990)(HL)**). The **'four unities'** are Possession, Interest, Title and Time:

- Possession: Each co-owner is as entitled to possession of each and every part of the land as any other. Unity of possession is the only unity present in both a joint tenancy and a tenancy in common.
- Interest: Each joint tenant must have the same interest in nature, eg, a freehold title and duration, eg, a fee simple.
- Title: Each joint tenant must acquire title from the same document or by the same act. Therefore, rights acquired under the same conveyance, or by simultaneous possession will suffice.
- Unity of Time: Each joint tenant's interest must vest, ie, take effect, at the same time.

10.06 Another important feature of the joint tenancy is the **right of survivorship** (*jus accrescendi*). As joint tenants are treated as if one person, where one dies, they are unable to pass their interest under their will, nor will it pass on intestacy (Administration of Estates Act 1925), but instead it accrues to the remaining joint tenants (**Re Caines (1978)**).

10.07 A **tenancy in common** exists where each of the co-owners has an **identifiable share, but it is undivided from the whole**, ie, 'an undivided share'. While the four unities are necessary for a joint tenancy to exist, only unity of possession is necessary for a tenancy in common.

10.08 In contrast to a joint tenancy, because a tenant in common has an identifiable, yet undivided share of the land, the interest can be left under a will and it will be effective, provided the will is validly executed (s9, Wills Act 1837). Equally, where there is no will, the rules on intestacy will operate to take the share to the next of kin of the deceased (Administration of Estates Act 1925).

Is there a Joint Tenancy or Tenancy in Common?

10.09   Well, legal title is easy, since this is **always a joint tenancy** (s1(6), LPA 1925), so it is never an issue how legal title is held. More complicated is equitable title, since this can be held as a joint tenancy or a tenancy in common. Thankfully, there are a number of things which you can look at to decide whether equitable title is a joint tenancy or a tenancy in common and these are: whether the four unities are present; whether there is an express declaration; where words of severance are used; and, whether a presumption operates.

Four Unities

10.10   Where the four unities of possession, interest, title and time are present, the equitable title will be held as a joint tenancy.

Express Declaration

10.11   Where the parties convey the land using express words, then the words in the conveyance will take effect (**Pink v Lawrence (1977)**).

Words of Severance

10.12   Where the conveyance contains words of severance, a tenancy in common may be found. Words of severance might be, eg, 'in equal shares' (**Payne v Webb (1874)**); 'equally' (**Re Kilvert (1957)**).

Presumptions

10.13   Equity operates a presumption against the joint tenancy; it distrusts the joint tenancy. Therefore, where property is purchased with unequal contributions of money, a tenancy in common will be found (**Bull v Bull (1955)**). Alternatively, where the relationship is a business, a tenancy in common will be found (**Lake v Craddock (1732)**). Finally, where there is nothing else to go on, the maxim *equity follows the law* operates to create a joint tenancy. However, presumptions can be rebutted by express words in the conveyance. In **R v Hayes (2018)(CA)**, the fact that one party provided all the purchase money did not negative a finding that the property was conveyed to the parties as joint tenants.

Severance

10.14   Where a joint tenancy is created, the right of survivorship operates to remove the possibility that a joint tenant might leave his interest by will on death (**Re Caines (1978)**). Therefore, in order to defeat the right of survivorship, the parties might **sever** their interest and thereby become tenants in common (**Harris v Goddard (1983)**). However, it should be remembered, **only an equitable joint tenancy can be severed**.

10.15   There are number of ways an equitable joint tenancy might be severed. Where equitable title is severed, the proportions are taken equally (**Goodman v Gallant (1986)(CA)**), unless the parties have contributed in unequal shares (**Bull v Bull (1955)(CA)**; **Stack v Dowden (2007)(HL)**), or agreed to some other form of division. Where severance is successful, it only severs the interest of the party severing. However, where there are only two joint tenants, and one severs, the whole of the joint tenancy is severed since the remaining party cannot be a joint tenant alone. Severance might be effected by:

1. Statutory written notice to other joint tenants;

2. Common law methods ('such other acts or things'):

(i) An act operating on its share;

(ii) Mutual agreement;

(iii) Mutual conduct.

3. Forfeiture as a means of severance.

1. Statutory written notice to other joint tenants

10.16   Under s36(2), LPA 1925 a joint tenant might sever the equitable estate by giving express written notice to the other joint tenants of their desire to sever the joint tenancy. The **written notice must manifest an immediate and irrevocable intention to sever (Re Draper's Conveyance (1969))**, and an intention to sever at some point in the future will not suffice (**Harris v Goddard (1983)(CA)**). No particular form of words is needed, nor is the notice required to be signed.

10.17   In order to be valid, the written notice under s36(2) must also be correctly served. Under s196, LPA 1925 certain conditions attach to correct service of the written notice. Under s196(3), LPA 1925, in order for service to be effective, the notice should be left at the last known abode or place of business of the other joint tenants, even if the notice is never read by the other joint tenant (**Kinch v Bullard (1999)**). Under s196(4), LPA 1925, service is deemed to have taken place when the written notice is posted in the pillar box and put into the postal system, so long as it is not returned 'could not be delivered'. (**Re 88 Berkley Road (1971)**).

2. Common law methods ('such other acts or things')

10.18   This is the common law set down in the case of **Williams v Hensman (1861)** and preserved by statute in s36(2), LPA 1925. The such other acts or things are:

(i)   An act operating on its share;

(ii)   Mutual agreement;

(iii)   Mutual conduct.

(i) Act operating on its share

10.19 This is an act by one of the joint tenants alone. Indeed, there is no need to inform the other joint tenants. Where a joint tenant becomes bankrupt (involuntary alienation), this severs their interest (**Re Gorman (1990)**), and their interest vests in a trustee in bankruptcy. Mortgaging (partial alienation) an interest also severs the joint tenancy (**Bedson v Bedson (1965)**). Finally, a sale or gift of the joint tenant's interest (total alienation), will sever the joint tenancy (**Brown v Raindle (1796)**).

(ii) Mutual agreement

10.20 Under this method of severance, the joint tenants reach an agreement to sever. The agreement has no need to reach any particular formality, and in the case of **Burgess v Rawnsley (1975)(CA)**, the agreement to sell was entirely oral. It does not have to be a specifically enforceable contract (**Hunter v Babbage (1994)**). However, it is clear that mere negotiations are not sufficient to effect severance by this method (**Gore and Snell v Carpenter (1990); Neilson-Jones v Fedden (1974)**).

(iii) Mutual conduct / 'course of dealing'

10.21 Under this method of severance, though the parties fail to reach agreement as to severance, their conduct is such that the joint tenancy is severed by the conduct. Severance by mutual conduct is rare and, indeed, the case law has often treated mutual agreement and mutual conduct as the same thing (see the judgment of Lord Denning MR in **Burgess v Rawnsley (1977)**).

10.22 Physical separation of the land by partition is not sufficient to effect severance of a joint tenancy (**Greenfield v Greenfield (1970)**). However, this might be restricted to its facts in that the judge found their joint intentions were relevant and that their intention was that the right of survivorship should continue to operate. However, an accepted method of severance is partition, which is, for example, separating one large parcel of land into two separate and distinct parcels of freehold. An order to this effect was made in **Ellison v Cleghorn (2013)**, where the intention had always been to segregate the titles from the outset when each joint owner was ready to build their own house.

3. Forfeiture as a means of severance

10.23 Where one joint tenant kills the other with the intention that they will benefit from the right of survivorship, such unlawful killing has the effect of severing the joint tenancy such that the killer cannot take the interest of the victim (**Re Crippen (1911)**).

Co-ownership – The Modern Statutory Framework

10.24 The key statute which governs the modern relationship between co-owners is the Trusts of Land and Appointment of Trustees Act ('ToLATA') 1996. Under s6, ToLATA 1996, the trustees under co-owned land have all the powers in dealing with the land of absolute owners. However, trustees remain subject to the rules of equity and the limitations placed on their actions by ToLATA 1996 where they are under an obligation to exercise their powers having regard to the rights of the beneficiaries (s6(5), ToLATA 1996). Additionally, the trustees are subject to the duty imposed by s1, Trustee Act 2000 to exercise reasonable care and skill.

10.25 In addition to these broad principles under ToLATA 1996, the Act is designed to settle disputes between co-owners as to sale of the land. Under ToLATA 1996, all land which is co-owned is held under a trust of land. However, under the old law, there was a presumption that land should be sold where there was a dispute as to sale. ToLATA 1996 creates no obligation to sell, but does give the power to any interested party to seek an order for sale. Where the trustees seek sale of the property to divide the proceeds between the beneficiaries, they must carry out consultations with the beneficiaries of full age and beneficially entitled to an interest in possession in the land (s11(1), ToLATA 1996) and, give effect to the wishes of the beneficiaries, or the majority (by value) where there is a dispute.

Co-ownership – ss14, 15 ToLATA 1996 and s335A, Insolvency Act 1986

10.26   Where there are disputes as to sale, etc, the mechanism for resolution of those disputes is provided by ToLATA 1996. Section 14, ToLATA 1996, any person with an interest, eg, trustee, beneficiary, mortgagee, or, trustee in bankruptcy, might make an application for sale. However, under ToLATA 1996, the court may make any order relating to the trustees' exercise of their functions, meaning, the court may make an order for sale or confirm the trustees must postpone sale until the occurrence of a specified event or may also make an order relieving them of any obligation to obtain the consent of or to consult any person in connection with the exercise of their functions (s14(2), ToLATA 1996). However, the most common form of s14 application will be an order for sale. Where the order for sale is sought by a beneficiary or a trustee, the court must take account of the guidelines in s15, ToLATA 1996. Where the application is by the trustee in bankruptcy, the court must consider the guidelines under s335A, Insolvency Act 1986.

s15, ToLATA 1996

10.27   The criteria under s15(3), ToLATA 1996 are:

(a) the intentions of the person(s) who created the trust;

(b) the purposes for which the trust property is to be held. For example, if the purpose endures, sale will not be ordered (**Re Buchanan-Wollaston's Conveyance (1939)**).

(c) the welfare of any minor who occupies or might reasonably be expected to occupy any land as his home;

(d) the interests of any secured creditor of any beneficiary.

10.28 Under s15(3), ToLATA, the circumstances and wishes of any beneficiaries of full age and, in dispute, those of the majority are also considered.

s335A, Insolvency Act 1986

10.29 Section 335A, Insolvency Act provides the court shall make such order as it thinks just and reasonable having regard to:

(a) the interests of the bankrupt's creditors;

(b) where the application is in respect of land that includes a dwelling house which is or has been the home of the bankrupt, his spouse or former spouse, the following criteria are taken into account:

(i) the conduct of the spouse or former spouse in so far as contributing to the bankruptcy;

(ii) the needs and financial resources of the spouse or former spouse; and

(iii) the needs of any children; and,

(c) all the circumstances of the case other than the needs of the bankrupt.

10.30 Criteria (b) and (c) can no longer be considered by the court after one year from bankruptcy, unless the circumstances are **exceptional**. After this period the interests of the bankrupt's creditors outweigh all other considerations.

10.31 What amounts to an exceptional circumstance must vary from case to case, but guidance might be taken from some cases decided under the provision. In **Re Citro (1991)**, forcing a wife and children to leave the family home was not exceptional, but displacing a party with mental illness (schizophrenia), would be **(Re Raval (1998))**. Likewise, an applicant with terminal cancer and only a limited time to live was deemed exceptional **(Re Bremner (1999))**.

CHAPTER 11
LEASES

Introduction

11.01   We have already looked at the characteristics of leases and how they are protected and binding on third parties in chapter two, paras 2.18 – 2.29 (inclusive). You may want to refresh your memory of this before reading the other important aspects of leases which we consider in this chapter. Those important additional elements of leases are **covenants** (the terms and conditions of a lease), and what happens when a lease or the freehold is transferred to a new owner – **will the covenants in the lease still be enforceable by and against the new owner of the lease?** The final part of the chapter considers remedies for breach of covenant and, particularly, forfeiture.

Covenants in Leases

11.02   The covenants in a lease are the obligations which the landlord and tenant each agree will be binding for the length of the lease. These covenants can be positive or negative, and they can vary significantly. Typical covenants include the **tenant's covenant to pay rent to the landlord**, or a covenant **not to use a residential premises for business purposes**. Generally, covenants are split into those which the landlord agrees, and those which the tenant agrees.

Landlord's Covenants

Quiet Enjoyment

11.03   A landlord agrees that the tenant should have **quiet enjoyment** of the premises for the length of the lease. This may be express or implied, and means that the landlord will allow the tenant possession of the premises, without interference from the landlord, for the duration of the lease (**Kenny v Preen (1963)**). In **Owen v Gadd (1956)**, the landlord was liable for erecting scaffolding around the premises which prevented the tenant from gaining access.

No derogation from grant

11.04   Once the lease has been granted, the landlord should not do something which would be inconsistent with the grant of the lease. In **Aldin v Latimer Clark Muirhead & Co (1894)**, a lease was taken for the purpose of using the premises for drying out timber, but the landlord was held to have derogated from grant by erecting buildings around the leased premises which interrupted the air flow needed to dry the tenant's timber.

Fitness for Human Habitation

11.05   A landlord is *generally* **not** under an obligation to let premises which are fit for human habitation (**Lane v Cox (1897)**), unless the premises has been let fully furnished, in which case it must be for human habitation at the start of the lease (**Wilson v Finch Hatton (1877)**).

Repair

11.06   A covenant to repair can, as a rule, be conferred on either party to a lease (**Cavalier v Pope (1906)**), but there is a notable exception for short leases, ie, **leases of less than seven years**. In such circumstances, ss11 – 14, Landlord and Tenant Act 1985, imposes a maintenance and repair obligation on the landlord. This relates to the structure and exterior of the building, and to keep utilities installations in repair, namely, water supply, gas, electricity, sanitation, etc. The lease cannot purport to exclude s11, Landlord and Tenant Act 1985.

Tenant's Covenants

Rates and Taxes

11.07　　The tenant is under an implied obligation to pay rates and taxes which fall due on the leased premises.

Damage or disrepair

11.08　　Tenants are under an obligation **not to commit waste**, meaning the tenant must avoid acts which alter the state of the land. **Voluntary waste** is something done deliberately to alter the land, eg, demolishing an internal wall. **Permissive waste** is something being left so that the premises is damaged. Linked to this is the obligation to **use the premises in a tenant-like manner (Warren v Keen (1954))**.

Permitting the landlord access

11.09　　The tenant should permit the landlord access to the premises to carry out repairs on the premises (**McGreal v Wake (1984)**).

Enforceability of Covenants

11.10　　What happens if the landlord sells their land (this is known as the **freehold reversion**) which is subject to a lease? Can the new owner enforce covenants against the tenant, or be liable for breach of the landlord's covenants? Alternatively, what happens if the tenant transfers (this is known as **assignment** or **assigning**) the lease to a new tenant? Can the new tenant enforce covenants which the landlord might have breached, and be held to covenants which the previous tenant agreed? Well, the short answer is that it depends on satisfaction of various rules, and when the lease in question was first granted. The **date the lease was first granted is important** because that will determine whether the **'old rules'** or the **'new rules'** apply to it. Let's start with the 'old rules'.

'Old rules'

11.11   For a lease which was granted before 1st January 1996, the 'old rules' apply. These rules are a mixture of common law and statute.

11.12   The starting point is to say that **all covenants agreed between the original landlord and the original tenant are enforceable between them as a matter of contract**, namely, the doctrine of privity of contract operates to make the enforceable. This includes personal as well as proprietary covenants. However, when either the freehold reversion or the lease change hands, only proprietary covenants are potentially enforceable.

'Old rules' – Landlord's sale of freehold reversion

11.13   Under **ss141** and **142, Law of Property Act 1925**, the benefit (s141) and the burden (s142) of the original lease, are enforceable by, and against, the new owner of the freehold reversion, provided it has **reference to the subject-matter of the lease**, meaning that the covenant is proprietary.

11.14   One slight quirk of these provisions is that the seller loses all his rights to enforce breaches of covenant which occurred while he was in possession, and they pass, instead, to the new landlord (**Re King (1963)**), including the right to sue for any unpaid rent (**Arlesford Trading Company Ltd v Servansingh (1971)**).

11.15   A further quirk of the old law is that the original tenant can enforce the lessor's covenants against the original landlord, even though the original landlord has sold the freehold reversion (**Stuart v Joy (1904)**). This is because of the **doctrine of privity of contract**.

'Old rules' – sub-tenants

11.16 What if the tenant sub-lets the property? In other words, they retain the main lease, but grant a third party a lease of a shorter period than their own. Can the main landlord (known as the 'head landlord') sue the sub-tenant for breaches of covenant which were agreed by the original tenant? Generally, the answer is 'no'. Why? Well, this is because there is no **privity of contract** between the head landlord and the sub-tenant, ie, they have no direct contractual relationship. Further, there is also no **privity of estate** between the head landlord and the sub-tenant.

11.17 However, though the answer is generally, 'no', there are exceptions: (i) Indirect enforcement; (ii) Restrictive covenants in the head lease.

(i)   Indirect enforcement

11.18 This is achieved by the head landlord suing the original tenant who, in turn, sues the sub-tenant. The reason the tenant can be sued is because they are responsible for the breaches committed by a sub-tenant under **s79, LPA 1925**.

(ii)   Restrictive covenants in the head lease

11.19 Where the covenant is restrictive, eg, states that a residential premises may not be used for business purposes, the **landlord may enforce the covenant directly against the sub-tenant (Hemingway Securities Ltd v Dunraven Ltd (1995))**. The conditions are taken from the case of **Tulk v Moxhay (1848)**, which is the case on enforceability of restrictive covenants in freehold land. You can look again at the detail in chapter four, paragraphs 4.21 – 4.27 (inclusive), but as a memory-refresher, these are:

> (i)   The covenant must be negative in substance;

> (ii)   The   covenant   must   accommodate   the

dominant tenement;

(iii) The original parties must have intended that the burden should bind successors;

(iv) The person against whom the covenant is being enforced must have notice of it.

'Old rules' – Tenants assignment of the lease

11.20 The transfer of a lease (known as an assignment) to a new tenant will allow covenants to be enforced provided certain conditions are satisfied. The conditions for enforcement are:

(i) There must be privity of estate, ie, a relationship of current landlord and current tenant;

(ii) It must be a legal lease;

(iii) The legal lease must have been legally assigned; AND,

(iv) The leasehold covenant must touch and concern the land.

(i) There must be privity of estate, ie, a relationship of current landlord and current tenant

11.21 There is **privity of estate** where there is a relationship of **current landlord and current tenant** between the landlord and the new tenant. This is easily satisfied.

(ii) It must be a legal lease

11.22 Where the lease has been created by deed and protected in the correct manner, or falls within the exception in s54(2), LPA 1925, the lease will be legal (**Boyer v Warby (1953)**).

(iii)   The legal lease must have been legally assigned

11.23   A legal lease is legally assigned by using a deed (s52 LPA 1925), which is a document which complies with s1, LP(MP)A 1989, meaning it is written, states on its face it is a deed, is signed by the grantor, witnessed, and delivered (dated). The lease will then need to be registered in the appropriate way.

(iv)   The leasehold covenant must touch and concern the land

11.24   This is the requirement that the covenant is one which affects the land, not one which is merely personal to the landlord and tenant.

'Old rules' – Continuing liability of tenant after assignment

11.25   As stated earlier, the original landlord remains liable throughout the lease. It is also the case that the original tenant remains liable on covenants in a pre-1996 lease (**Allied London Ltd v Hambro Ltd (1984)**), even after assignment of the lease. Thus, the original tenant may be liable for breaches committed by the new tenant. In such circumstances, the original tenant may look for means of getting their money back from the new tenant. Fortunately, the original tenant does have some options.

11.26   First, they could rely on the **law of unjust enrichment (Moule v Garrett (1872))** which requires that the original tenant be reimbursed by the new tenant for any costs incurred by the original tenant because the new tenant breached the leasehold covenants.

11.27   Secondly, the original tenant might rely on either **sch 12, para 20, Land Registration Act 2002**, which **implies an indemnity covenant** into the assignment of the lease, where title to the lease is registered, or a similar provision in **s77, Law of Property Act 1925**, where title to the lease is unregistered.

'New rules' – Landlord and Tenant (Covenants) Act 1995

11.28   This statute applies to **all leases granted on or after 1st January 1996**, and makes quite radical changes to the 'old rules', discussed above.

11.29   Under the 1995 Act, the **original tenant is automatically released from the burden of leasehold covenants when lease is assigned (s5, LT(C)A 1995)**. The landlord is not, however, automatically released from the burden of covenants, but may serve a notice of release (**s6, LT(C)A 1995**) on the tenant with a request, but this has been doubted by (**London Diocesan Fund v Avonridge Property Company Limited (2005)(HL)**).

11.30   Further, covenants **no longer** *need to touch and concern* or *have reference to the subject-matter of the lease* to pass **(ss2 and 3, LT(C)A 1995)**. The **benefit and burden** of all leasehold covenants pass automatically on assignment of the lease or transfer of the freehold reversion, unless they are expressed to be personal (**First Penthouse v Channel Hotels and Properties (2003)**). It is also the case that the anomalous case of **Re King (1963)**, discussed at 11.14, above, is reversed for "new" leases (**s24(4), LT(C)A 1995**).

Authorised Guarantee Agreements ('AGA')

11.31   Though it is the case that under the LT(C)A 1995, the original tenant is released from the burden of covenants when they assign the lease, the landlord, as a condition of assignment, can require the new tenant to enter into an **authorised guarantee agreement** ('AGA') (**s16, LT(C)A 1995**). Under an AGA, the original tenant agrees to guarantee the performance, by the new tenant, of the covenants under the lease. If the lease is assigned again, the AGA agreed by the original tenant is **automatically discharged**.

11.32 A tenant may only enter into an AGA where the landlord demonstrates that there is a qualified or absolute prohibition on assignment in the lease and that any consent to assignment of the lease is given subject to the condition that the tenant assigning the lease enters into an AGA.

11.33 Merely entering into an AGA does not mean that the tenant is wholly exposed to the wrongdoing of the new tenant, since s17, LT(C)A 1995 states that the landlord must serve notice within six months of any unpaid rent becoming due, stating the amount owed. Any tenant who has to **pay the arrears of a new tenant has the right to be granted an overriding lease (s19, LT(C)A 1995)** for a **term equal to the remainder of the tenancy plus three days**. An overriding lease essentially allows the original (old) tenant to become the landlord of the current tenant, which gives the holder of the overriding lease the power to forfeit the lease and prevent other breaches by injunction.

11.34 These provisions of the LT(C)A 1995 are **retrospective**, and **apply to old leases and new leases**.

Tenant's Remedies for Landlord's Breach of Covenant

11.35 A tenant has a range of remedies available where a landlord is in breach of covenant. First, the tenant might claim an **injunction** against the landlord which either prevents a threatened breach of trust (a **prohibitory injunction**), or forces the landlord to undertake repairs where, for example, they are under a statutory obligation to repair, as under s11, Landlord and Tenant Act 1985. An injunction which forces the landlord to do something is a **mandatory injunction**. As an alternative to a mandatory injunction, a tenant might also ask for the remedy of **specific performance** against the landlord. This equitable remedy requires an individual to perform the positive obligations under a lease. Importantly, **s17, Landlord and Tenant Act 1985** confirms that the remedies of mandatory injunction and specific performance are available in relation to the landlord's repairing obligation, but that the usual bars on equitable remedies do not operate.

11.36 Further remedies include a claim for **damages for breach of covenant**, which are assessed on the basis of the loss which the tenant has suffered, eg, from moving out and having to pay rent for alterative accommodation while repairs are carried out. Finally, the tenant may **repudiate** the lease, treating it as being at an end (**Hussein v Mehlman (1992)**).

Landlord's Remedies for Tenant's Breach of Covenant

11.37 The landlord's remedies available against the tenant vary depending on what covenant has been breached: whether the covenant is the rent, or the non-rent, covenant.

Remedies for non-payment of rent

11.38 If the tenant has not paid the rent, then the remedy of an **action for recovery of the debt** will be available. The ancient remedy of **distraint** was abolished by Part 3, Tribunals, Courts and Enforcement Act 2007, and replaced with a scheme to operate in relation to commercial leases only, namely the Commercial Rent Arrears Recovery scheme, which came into force on 6th April 2014.

11.39 Alternatively, a landlord may **forfeit the lease** for non-payment of rent. **Forfeiture**, is the remedy of the landlord **taking the lease back and bringing an end to the landlord and tenant relationship**. In order to forfeit a lease, there must be a forfeiture clause in the lease; without one, the lease may not be forfeited. It may be achieved by **peaceful re-entry** of the premises, or by **court order**. Note, it may only be by court order where the premises is residential.

11.40 The tenant may seek relief from forfeiture, that is, they may seek to reverse the forfeiture action by the landlord. If under the jurisdiction of the County Court, then the tenant must make their application within six months of the date on which the landlord recovered possession (s138(9A), County Courts Act 1984), where possession was made by court order, or within six months of the date of the landlord taking possession (s139, CCA 1984) (**Golding v Martin (2019)(CA)**). If under the jurisdiction of the High Court, and forfeiture was by court order, an application must be made within six months of execution of the judgment (s38(1), Senior Courts Act 1981; s210, Common Law Procedure Act 1852). Where by peaceful re-entry, the court may grant relief under its inherent jurisdiction (**Billson v Residential Apartments (1992)(CA)**), but there is no set limitation period, but it is likely to be subject to any consideration of delay.

11.41 In October 2019, the Supreme Court in **Manchester Ship Canal Co Ltd v Vauxhall Motors Ltd**, held that it was possible to seek relief from forfeiture where something other than a proprietary right was held by the claimant. Thus, the Court permitted relief from forfeiture of a licence held by Vauxhall Motors Ltd.

Remedies for breach of non-rent covenants

11.42 A landlord may claim an injunction or specific performance against the tenant for breach of covenant, as discussed, above, at para 11.36, though specific performance is a rarely used remedy against a tenant from the landlord's perspective. Further, the landlord may also bring an action for damages against the tenant for breach of covenant, assessed on the basis of the loss which the landlord has suffered (18, Landlord and Tenant Act 1927; Leasehold Property (Repairs) Act 1938).

11.43 The landlord may also **forfeit** the lease from breach of a covenant other than a rent covenant. The procedure is provided in **s146, Law of Property Act 1925**, which requires that a notice be served:

(i)   Specifying the breach which has occurred; and,

(ii) If capable of remedy, require that it be remedied within a reasonable time; and,

(iii) Require the tenant to pay compensation if required.

11.44 If the breach is not remedied, then the landlord may forfeit by **court order** or **peaceful re-entry**. Some breaches are incapable of remedy, such as those which place a taint on the land. For example, use of the leased premises for immoral purposes in **Governors of Rugby School v Tannahill (1935)** is not capable of remedy.

11.45 It should be noted that a right of re-entry must have arisen before a s146 notice is served (**Toms v Ruberry (2019)(CA)**).

11.46 The tenant may apply for discretionary relief from forfeiture under **s146(2), Law of Property Act 1925**. The exercise of the discretion will depend on the circumstances of the case.

Termination of a Lease

11.47 A lease may be terminated by the **passage of time**; the term simply comes to an end, or by a **break clause** contained in the lease which allows the landlord or tenant to bring the lease to a premature conclusion. Equally, a lease may come to an end by **surrender**, or by **merger**, as where the tenant acquires the freehold. Finally, as stated, it may also come to an end by **forfeiture**.

CHAPTER 12
ADVERSE POSSESSION

Introduction

12.01   As already indicated, while land law generally requires formality in the acquisition of estates and interests in land, in some circumstances estates and interests might be acquired informally, and **adverse possession is an instance of informal acquisition**.

12.02   In order to acquire title to land by adverse possession, the claimant must satisfy a mixture of **common law** and **statutory rules**: whether adverse possession has occurred is a matter of satisfying the common law; whether the requisite period of possession has been completed is a question of statute.

Has adverse possession occurred?

12.03   In order to show adverse possession, the claimant must demonstrate:

(i)   Factual possession (*factum possessionis*); AND,

(ii)   Intention to possess (*animus possidendi*)

JA Pye (Oxford) Ltd v Graham (2003)(HL)

12.04   Though these are separate requirements, they overlap heavily and **intention can often be found** by looking at the **factual possession (JA Pye (Oxford) Ltd v Graham (2003)(HL))**. Indeed, the practical approach is to look at all the circumstances of the claim (**Smart v Lambeth BC (2013)(CA)**). Each requirement is, nevertheless, considered separately.

(i)   Factual possession (factum possessionis)

12.05   The factual possession required must endure for the relevant period of adverse possession and whether it is successful will depend on the facts; it is truly fact sensitive. What is clear, however, is that the possession should not be because of a lease, licence, or any other form of consent. Permission, or the acknowledgement that someone has a better title than you claim, will defeat the claim (**Lambeth LBC v Archangel (2002)**). However, a willingness to pay rent if challenged will not defeat the claim (**JA Pye (Oxford) Ltd v Graham (2003)(HL)**).

12.06   A good measure of the sort of behaviour which might amount to the required factual possession can be taken from the cases. For example, in the leading case of **JA Pye (Oxford) Ltd v Graham (2003)(HL)**, grazing cattle and padlocking the gated access to the land and retaining the key were sufficient. Equally, erecting fences (**Wimpey Ltd v Sohn (1967)**), and security cameras and lighting (**Prudential Assurance Ltd v Waterloo Real Estate (1999)**) will also suffice.

12.07   In the recent case of **Thorpe v Frank (2019)(CA)**, the paving of an open area in front of a bungalow, without fencing around the entire area, was also sufficient factual possession, especially as the paving of the adversely possessed area matched that which the claimant already owned.

12.08   These acts, of themselves, are quite significant. It stands to reason, therefore, that minimal acts will not meet the necessary level of factual possession (**Hounslow LBC v Minchinton (1997)**).

(ii)   Intention to possess (animus possidendi)

12.09   The intention needed is the **intention to possess**, not the intention to own (**Buckinghamshire CC v Moran (1990)**), but part of that intention is the exclusion of the whole world, including the actual owner (**Powell v McFarlane**

(1977)).

12.10   Quite often, intention can be inferred from the conduct of the person in possession. As stated earlier, there can be overlap between intention and factual possession, and drawing intention from conduct is an instance of that.

12.11   One thing is clear, namely that the intention to possess must be clear, so that anyone observing the possession, even the owner, would grasp that someone else was in possession of the land (**Powell v McFarlane (1977)**).

The Clock

12.12   Once factual possession and intention to possess are established, the claimant must demonstrate that they have been in possession of the land for the correct length of time. Generally, this will depend on whether title to the land is registered or unregistered. There are three schemes:

(i)   adverse possession where title is unregistered;

(ii)   adverse possession of registered title under the old law;

(iii)   adverse possession of registered title under the new law

12.13   Before we consider those three, it should be noted at what point the clock starts to 'tick'. Well, it starts once the owner has been dispossessed, or abandoned possession.

(i)   adverse possession where title is unregistered

12.14   The period of adverse possess in unregistered title is 12 years (s15, Limitation Act 1980), and the clock runs from the moment of adverse possession. After the requisite period is complete, the owner's title is extinguished, and the possessor's title is superior (**Buckinghamshire CC v Moran (1990)**).

12.15   The successful possessor does, however, take the property subject to all pre-existing legal and equitable rights, whether registered under Land Charges Act 1972 or not.

12.16   If the title possessed is a leasehold, the extinguishing of title relates only to the tenant's estate, not the landlord's estate.

(ii)   adverse possession of registered title under the old law

12.17   It is worth stating that this is now unlikely to arise as time passes, but if the title possessed is registered and the period of 12 years was completed before 13th October 2003, then the possessor is entitled to be registered as the proprietor of the land.

(iii)   adverse possession of registered title under the new law

12.18   The modern scheme of adverse possession where title is registered is to be found in the Land Registration Act 2002. The new law makes it more difficult to obtain a registered title by adverse possession.

12.19   First, there is no automatic limitation period, therefore no loss of title merely by passage of a fixed period of time (s96, LRA 2002), even if the claimant is able to show factual possession and an intention to possess. What happens now is governed by schedule 6, LRA 2002. After 10 years, a claimant may apply to be registered and if the Registrar thinks there is an arguable case for registration, a notice is sent to the current registered proprietor (sch 6, para 2, LRA 2002).

12.20   Once the notice is received, the registered owner may consent, object, or serve a counter-notice.

ABOUT THE AUTHOR

I'm a law lecturer with over 20 years' experience of teaching and explaining the law at undergraduate and postgraduate levels. I have tutored students in both the public and private sectors, at old and new universities, across a range of subjects, including land law.

Printed in Great Britain
by Amazon

19656258R00068